South Lancashire

Edited by Sarah Marshall

 Young**Writers**

First published in Great Britain in 2005 by:
Young Writers
Remus House
Coltsfoot Drive
Peterborough
PE2 9JX
Telephone: 01733 890066
Website: www.youngwriters.co.uk

SB ISBN 1 84602 159 6

Foreword

Young Writers was established in 1991 and has been passionately devoted to the promotion of reading and writing in children and young adults ever since. The quest continues today. Young Writers remains as committed to the fostering of burgeoning poetic and literary talent as ever.

This year's Young Writers competition has proven as vibrant and dynamic as ever and we are delighted to present a showcase of the best poetry from across the UK. Each poem has been carefully selected from a wealth of *Playground Poets* entries before ultimately being published in this, our thirteenth primary school poetry series.

Once again, we have been supremely impressed by the overall high quality of the entries we have received. The imagination, energy and creativity which has gone into each young writer's entry made choosing the best poems a challenging and often difficult but ultimately hugely rewarding task - the general high standard of the work submitted amply vindicating this opportunity to bring their poetry to a larger appreciative audience.

We sincerely hope you are pleased with our final selection and that you will enjoy *Playground Poets South Lancashire* for many years to come.

Contents

Erin Middleton (10)   14
Charles Butterworth (9)   14
Becci Byrne (9)   14
Luke Collins (9)   15
Sam Hardacre (9)   15
Chloe Tomson (10)   15
Emma Dowd (10)   16
Chantelle Kennedy (9)   16
Ashley Haggart (9)   16
Tom Withers (9)   17
Richard Davies (8)   17
Alexander McNicholas (9)   17
Musa Khan (9)   18
Taryn Mallison (9)   18
Paige Owens (8)   18
Sally Jones (10)   18
Jake Howard (11)   19
Adam Fitton (11)   19
Thomas Hopkinson (8)   19
Lydia Stanton (8)   19
Ross Belch (9)   20
Adam Hargreaves (11)   20
Daniel Lewis (10)   20
Abigail Taylor-Spencer (9)   21
Katherine Burton (8)   21
Alana Grundy (9)   21
Melissa Bailey (9)   22
Rachel Moscrop (8)   22
Rachel Flynn (8)   22
Victoria Newman (9)   22
Joseph Royle (9)   23
Abigail Higham (9)   23
Matthew Davis (9)   24

Christ Church CE Walshaw Primary School

Robyn Bailey (9)   24
Luke Benson (10)   24
Lydia Instone (9)   25
Darryl Owen (9)   26
Madeleine McCann (10)   26
Bethany Rawcliffe (9)   27

Amber-Rose Perry (9)   28
Edmund Farrell (10)   28
Samantha Lees (10)   ·29
Jessica Duckworth (9)   30
Hollie Vizard (10)   30
Rebecca Sandford (9)   31
Ashley Pickstone (10)   31
Megan Howard (10)   32
David Stewart (10)   33
Ethan Turner (9)   33
Lucy Heys (9)   34
Natasha Hamilton (10)   34
Amy Warner (9)   35
Joshua Redgrave (9)   35
Lucy Allen-Baines (8)   36
Jonathon Berry (9)   36
Lisa McDermott (8)   37
Remesha Sutherland (8)   37
Sian Devine (8)   38
Rachel Taylor (8)   38
Lara Sugden (8)   39
Ashley Brooks (8)   39
Jonathan Barnes (8)   40
Joshua Brownlow (9)   40
James Dutka (8)   41
Mylo Dougherty (8)   41
Ailisha Cooper (8)   42
Ross Allen (8)   42

Guardian Angels' RC Primary School

Joe Geeling (10)   42
Victoria McCauley (11)   43
Dominic Anderson (11)   43
Sophie Balmbra (10)   44
Natasia Coote (10)   44
Rebecca Hajdukewycz (11)   45
Lauren Doughty (11)   45
Beth Banim (10)   46
Rebecca Cooper (11)   46
Charlotte McDonald (11)   47
Alexander Hall (11)   47

Heskin Pemberton CE Primary School

Highfield St Matthew's CE Primary School

Jade Nolan (11)	63
Molly Selby (11)	63
Melissa Jones (8)	64
James McHugh (10)	64
David Griffiths-Naylor (9)	64
Jade Cartwright (11)	65
Alexandra Jo Clark (8)	65
Andrew Saxon (8)	66
Sean Hewitt (8)	66
Lauren Melling (8)	67
Sophie Brown (8)	67
Kayleigh Anderson (9)	68
Leah Coates (9)	68
Sophie Atherton (9)	69
Thomas Wheeler (8)	69
Abbie Whelan (9)	69
Jack Macdonald (9)	70
Daniel McNamara (8)	70
Liam Heaton (8)	71
Matthew Price (8)	71
Amy Barlow (8)	71
Archie Selby (8)	72
Joshua Steven Gannon (8)	72
Cara Aston (8)	72
Alexandra Rayner (9)	72
Janet Waterworth (9)	73
Samantha Brown (9)	73
Jamie Carney (8)	73
Jason Williams (9)	73
Aaron Sibblies (11)	74
Ashley Gregory (11)	74
Adam Murphy (10)	75
Bradley Price (8)	75
Georgia Ascroft (8)	76
Johnathan Massey (10)	76
Laura Rebecca Adamson (10)	77
Amy Duckworth (8)	77
Alisha Bartolini (8)	77
Rebecca Davies (10)	78
Joshua Cooke (9)	78
Sarah Butler (10)	78
Alexander Clarke (9)	78

Deryn Jones (10)	79
Alex Liptrot (9)	79
Christopher Rosbotham (10)	80
Zoe Greenall (10)	80
Ashleigh Wiggin (10)	80
Lauren Lindley (9)	81
Emilie Welsby (9)	81
Luke Sheridan (9)	81
Jack Aspey (7)	82
Samantha Critchley (8)	82
Rebecca Howard (9)	82
Katie Shore (9)	83
Zak Miller (8)	83
Reece Hampson (8)	83
Dayna Leanne Clark (8)	83

Holy Infant & St Anthony RC Primary School

Christian Hardman (10)	84
Matthew McGrath (9)	84
Georgia Beaman (10)	85
Elizabeth Hamer (10)	85
Bethany Nuttall (10)	86
Michael Taylor (10)	86
Belinda Nicholson (10)	86
Joshua Haddock (11)	87
Naomi Sarsfield (11)	87
Megan Andrews (10)	88
Rebecca Wood (10)	88
Sarah Shilson (11)	89
Eric Holliday (11)	89
Briony Grant (10)	90
Laura Wright (11)	90
Jessica Pendlebury (10)	91
Leonie Hazelwood (9)	91
Chelsie Conaghan (11)	92
Alexandra Kelly (9)	92
Zak Riding (8)	93
Thomas McNair (10)	93
Sean Mulheran (9)	93
Hannah Castley (10)	94
Jessica Flannery Maloney (10)	94

Luke Naylor (9)	94
Alex Forbes (9)	95
Nicole Holliday (10)	95
Jessica Ratcliffe (9)	96
Georgie Lynam (9)	96
Jason Nicholson (8)	96
Shannon Boyce (9)	97
Dillon Sandiford (9)	97
Georgina Killeen (8)	97
Luke Barber (8)	98
Bethany Taberner (9)	98
Adam Liptrott (9)	98
Adam Lee Reynolds (11)	99
Nicole Jones (11)	99
Ryan Kelly (11)	99
Elizabeth Shepherd (10)	100

Moorside Community Primary School

James Rogers (9)	100
Benjamin Hyman (7)	100
Lauren Gaskell (9)	101
Georgia Gaskell (9)	101
Jack Lewis (9)	102
Kieran Reason (9)	102
Keyleigh Storey (9)	103
Aaron Smith (9)	103
Lauren Bullock (9)	104
Shannon Jenkins (8)	104
Zoe Flannery (8)	105
Daniel Hallam (9)	105
Kyle Doherty (10)	106
Kane Magrath (7)	106
Kyle Weedall (11)	106
Corey Hardiman (9)	107
Luke Weedall (11)	107
Carl Wright (10)	107
Daniella Dreha (10)	108
Fern Roberts (8)	108
Reece Taylor (9)	109
Erin Wells-Lakeland (9)	109
Kimberley Gaskell (9)	110

Nicole Marsh (10)   128
Hannah Bethell (10)   128
Sophie Whittle (10)   129
Heather Lamb (7)   129
Abigail Preston (8)   130
James Morris (8)   130
Amber Edmundson (8)   131
Ben Possible (9)   131
Matthew Seddon (8)   132
Joshua Knowles (8)   132
Tanya Bass (9)   133
Alex Morris (9)   133
Eleanor McVey (8)   134
Eleanor Strang (8)   134
Emma Harrison (9)   135
Bethany Hughes (8)   135
Roseanna Feeney (7)   136
Kelly Nightingale (8)   136
Chloe Townsend (9)   137

St John's RC Primary School, Bolton

Elliot Saunders (9)   137
Tara Vinden (9)   138
Bradley Marlor (8)   138
Tejal Shanbhag (8)   139
Charlotte Howarth (8)   139
Oliver Burns (8)   140
Liam Ryan (8)   140
Phillipa Tinker (8)   141
Matthew Clarkson (8)   141
Victoria Rozdziabyk (9)   141
Emma Hunt (8)   142
Nicole Rodgers (9)   142
Jacob Cooper (8)   142
Rebecca Povall (8)   143
Sean McQuaid (8)   143
Ellie Edginton (8)   143
Jack Cullen (8)   144
Thomas Pilling (8)   144
Peter McGowan (9)   144
Brittany Bennett (8)   145

Tom Greenhalgh (8)   145
Emily Unsworth (8)   145
Emilee Fullaway (9)   146
Daniel Hill (8)   146

St Mark's CE Primary School, Ormskirk
Sam Rooney (10)   147
Emily Gibbs (9)   147
Calum Williams (10)   148
Olivia McCoombe (9)   148

St Mary's Catholic Primary School, Scarisbrick
Ashley Oldfield (9)   148
Alexander Blundell (10)   149
Steven Ashton (11)   149
Liam Hesketh (11)   149
Max Hindle (10)   150
Georgia Berry (9)   150
Robert Hilton (10)   150
Alex Alderdice (10)   151
Nicole Cronin (10)   151
Elliot Ryder (10)   151
Wallace Louise Berry (11)   152
Frank Sharratt (9)   152
Adam Jordan (9)   152
George Sargent (10)   153

St Mary's CE Primary School, Hawkshaw, Bury
Ejiro Kevu (11)   153
Josh Dudley (8)   153
Stephanie Belk (9)   154
Jordan Tipping (9)   154
Courteney Kiely (8)   155
Joseph Phillips (10)   155
Tom Robinson (10)   155
Guy Loxham (9)   156
Hamish Fraser Fleming (7)   156
Adam Purves (10)   156
Nicole Rigby (8)   157
Shannon Wilkinson (9)   157
Courtney Freeman (10)   157

Lisanne Mallinder (10)	158
Rebecca Pearson (9)	158
Hollie Ashworth (11)	159
Ese Kevu (8)	159
Conor O'Neill (9)	159
Emily Baker (11)	160
Victoria Hui (10)	160
Harry Edward Dixon (8)	160
Bethany Smith (10)	161
Georgina Gloster (7)	161
Madeline Allanson (8)	161
Molly Phillips (8)	162
Kate Smith (7)	162
Lars Christopherson (7)	162
Jessica Bailey (9)	163
Bethany Kay (8)	163
Sadie Grecian (10)	163
Jade Johnston (10)	164
Alex Walker (8)	164
Eleanor Hamer (8)	165

St Peter's CE Primary School, Bury

Iqra Asghar (10)	165
Liam Wood (10)	165
Darcey Pearson (10)	166
Jodie Thornley (9)	166
David Rimmer (9)	166
Dani Marshall (11)	167
Leah Shepley (10)	167
Rachael Walsh (9)	167
Lauren Dixon (10)	168
Sarah Littler (10)	168
Thomas Ridgley (9)	168
Aston Roger (9)	169
James Wrethman (10)	169
Ryan Heslop (10)	170
Louise Cunliffe (11)	170
Jenna Vaughan (10)	171
Afsheen Jamil (9)	171
Sarah Green (9)	172
Jack Harris (10)	172

Conor Duthie (9)	173
Sophie Whittaker (9)	173
Sophie Mansell (10)	174
Jack Haigh (9)	174
Joshua Whittaker (10)	174
Gabrielle Wilson (10)	175
Emma Hanley (10)	175
Dayna Crabtree (10)	176
Lauren McDonald (9)	176
Becky Torr (10)	177
Hayley Turner (10)	178
Lauren Howard (10)	179

St Simon & St Jude's CE Primary School, Bolton

Chanice Patel (9)	179
Ashleigh Barghuti (8)	180
Mehran Mokri (9)	180
Nadia Harman (8)	181
Daniella Seddon (8)	181
Amber Barlow (8)	182
Hafsa Iqbal (8)	182
Kishan Patel (7)	182
Irram Amjad (8)	183

Whittle-Le-Woods CE Primary School

Roisin Wherry (9)	183
Sarah Hanrahan (10)	183
Jessica Murphy (10)	184
Charlene Broomhead (10)	184
Isabelle Kennedy (10)	185
Hannah Vickerman (9)	185
Josie Hull (8)	186
Emma Davies (9)	186
Sam Mundy (10)	187
Charlotte Kenyon (10)	187
Heidi Clement (7)	188
Samantha Edwards (10)	189
Eleanor Gibson (8)	190
Joshua Mansfield (11)	191
Lucy Gaskell (7)	192
Dayna Bateman (8)	193

Katie Smith (10)	193
Rhiannon Bennett (7)	194
Emma Galloway (8)	195
Jack Gowan (9)	195
Samuel Mansfield (8)	196
Aashay Vaidya (11)	197
Chelsie Humber (11)	197
Rachel Hanrahan (8)	198
Laura Hannett (8)	199
Nicole Richardson (7)	200
Emma Pearson (11)	201
Kate McMullan (7)	202
Liam Pearse (9)	203
Owen Grimes (7)	204
Emily Flewitt (10)	205
Lily Dickinson (9)	205
Quine Skillen (7)	206
Chelsie Heyworth (9)	207
Holly Magill (9)	207
Jack Strong (8)	208
Martin Parry (9)	209
Keira Skillen (9)	209
Robson Broomhead (7)	210
James Booth (10)	211
Megan Downs (8)	212
Evie Sanderson (10)	212
Kathryn Unsworth (11)	213
Madeline Fisher (9)	213
Georgina Russell (11)	214
Hannah Smith-Haughton (9)	214
April Bateman (11)	215
Alice Gregory (8)	216

Withnell Fold Primary School

Ben Lancaster (9)	217
Natalie Toth (10)	218
Elizabeth Jones (11)	219
Shona Jackson (10)	219
Natasha McMahon (10)	220
Bethany Wood (10)	221
Ali Wrigley (10)	222

The Poems

I See The Sea

The sea, the sea
As gentle as can be
Sometimes soft
Sometimes rough
Hardly ever tough
But when it gets rather nasty
It's as deadly as killer needles
The sea is there
I see the sea
Everybody loves the sea
Not just me
The sea is the colour of a whale's back
Lifting past the night sky
The waves will never lie
Waves are pupils of the sea
They protect the sea at all costs
We're going home to Battersea
I don't see the sea!

Alex Tighe (10)
Asmall Primary School

The Sea

The sea is a calm, gentle giant
Rippling its waves upon the rocks
Boundless to all creatures
Pulling his treasures back to him
This is the sea.

The sea smashes into the rocks
Clinging to the vast high cliffs
Dragging creatures to their death
All that's left is the dull, yellow sand
This is sea.

Jake Duff (10)
Asmall Primary School

The Sea

The sea is a ripper
The sea is a killer
The sea is rough
The sea is a ginormous giant
With an empty belly, after you
The sea is hungry
Hungry for people

The sea is a sleeping baby
The sea is a tiger
Waiting to pounce
The sea is the sea . . .
A mood changer.

Stephen Coleman (11)
Asmall Primary School

The Stormy Sea

The stormy sea, the stormy sea,
Thunder and lightning let it be.
It can be quiet, it can be loud
Rain and hail and stormy clouds.
Blundering, thunder lights up the sky,
Look at that stray ship getting wrecked -
Is it yours or mine?
Soon after, the storm dies down
Have a look and you will see
Nothing more than a frown
Just after the stormy sea.

Jack Evans (10)
Asmall Primary School

What Is The Sea?

The sea is a beautiful queen with a talented voice,
The sea is a wicked king with a terrible anger.
The sea is a huge, turquoise blanket that covers you from head to toe.
The sea is a horrible monster ready to gobble you up.
The sea is a furry little kitten, playing with a yarn of wool,
The sea is a gigantic dog, slobbering all over you
And putting his wet, soggy paws on your lap.

The sea is a lot of things, good and bad!

Hannah Bober (11)
Asmall Primary School

The Sea

The sea is as blue as a dolphin's back,
The sea is as calm as a pond,
The sea is as rough as a hedgehog's back,
The sea is as long as an enormous snake,
The sea howls like a dog,
The sea pounces on our stuff,
The sea tears down houses and trains,
The sea never changes, but is always different.

John Edwards (11)
Asmall Primary School

The Sea

The sea is a hungry monster coming after you.
The sea is a comforting turquoise blanket.
The sea is a powerful king that rules the ocean.
The sea can be amazing or cruel.
The sea can be a starved dog, barking for some food.
The sea, the sea, the sea,
Just look at the sea.

Matthew Smith (9)
Asmall Primary School

The Sea

It's a huge monster ready to swallow you up
It's a blue wavy desert, which lasts forever
It roars when it is really angry
It whispers in its sleep
It tossed you into the air
It's a comfortable, blue bed, which you can lie on
It's got a loud roar that can deafen you
It howls in the fierce wind
It eats all the rumbling, tumbling stones
It has all the sea creatures in it
It moans and groans for more stones
It is like an underwater city
Deep in the murky depths of the ocean
That is the sea!

Ben Darcy (9)
Asmall Primary School

The Sea

There are waves that crash and waves that pounce.
There are waves that are deadly and waves that are calm.
Waves to run away from.
Waves to play and paddle in.
Waves that are blue and waves that are green.
Waves that are freezing cold
Waves that are big and waves that are small.
But most of all, the sea will never end,
Waves go on forever.

Noel Williams (10)
Asmall Primary School

Waves

Waves that are big
Waves that are small
Waves that chase you to the seabed
Waves that rock you to sleep
Waves that spin you into the air
Waves that curl over into the air
Waves that look at you like an angry dog
Waves that are small, but violent
Waves coming to land
Waves that glide along the sea's flow
Waves that grab you from behind
Waves that shake you
Waves that shock you at any time
Waves that take you.

Bobby Williams (11)
Asmall Primary School

The Sea

The sea is a giant turquoise blanket,
Covering up a yellow mattress.
The sea is a rubbish dump,
Eating everything given to it.
The sea is an endangered creature,
Running away from hunters on land.
The sea is a huge pool of water,
Held in God's hand!

Tamaris Higham (11)
Asmall Primary School

The Sea Show

Come see the sea show,
The greatest show in town.
Come see the sea show,
Everyone gather round!

It's time for the sea show,
Is everybody here?
It's time for the sea show,
Are you sitting comfortably my dear?

First come the schools of fish,
Dancing in their groups,
Next come the dolphins,
Jumping through their hoops!

Now here are the mermaids,
Elegantly swimming around,
Look it's the blue whale,
Squirting out his fountain.

Last here come the waves,
Rippling for you,
What a show! What a show!
But wait there's more.

Now here is everyone,
For the grand finale,
Wow I loved that show,
I'm seeing that again.

Megan Rainbird (9)
Asmall Primary School

The Tidal Wave

Running, running for my life, I thought that I was going to die.
All that I could hear was the terrifying sea roaring at me.

That was my worst nightmare, I thought it was a dream.
Sadly it wasn't.
It was breathtaking.
It was a monster chasing me down the beach.

People were staring at me eagerly.
I got even more scared.
It was like the beach was growing as I was running.

Suddenly I tripped. The wave grabbed me.
Before I knew it I was lying on the beach.
Dead!

Amanda Lewis (10)
Asmall Primary School

The Playground

Playtime's fun,
By the sun.
People bad,
Teachers mad.
Kick the ball,
At the wall,
People eat toast,
While the ball hits the post.
Bells ringing,
Birds singing,
Whistle blows,
Doors close.

Lee Bebb (10)
Brookfield Park Primary School

The Playground

The playground is fun,
The playground is sad,
They fit together and come out mad.

Some are happy,
Some are bad,
When the bell rings
The teacher is glad.

Luke Manley (10)
Brookfield Park Primary School

The Playground

At playtime it's fun time,
For screaming and chatting.
Playing with your friends is so much fun
When you're smiling with the sun.
Whether you're playing football or skipping,
It still makes a playtime good.
But then you have to say bye-bye to the sun.

Jennifer Sweeney (10)
Brookfield Park Primary School

Playtime

At playtime it's the coldest time ever.
At playtime I shiver and freeze.
I do so hate the breeze.

You want to come into the warm.
'You have to stay out!' the teachers scream.

Christopher Cheeseman (8)
Brookfield Park Primary School

The Playground

The playground is huge,
The playground is small,
The playground is loud,
It's so much fun.
Soon it ends we have to work.
When it's play again, it's OK.
Soon the noise starts again.

Ryan Finegan (9)
Brookfield Park Primary School

Playground

The playground is noisy
The playground is loud
So blow the whistle
To keep the noise down.

Children screaming and shouting around,
The poor old teacher doesn't like the sound.

Rebecca Angell (9)
Brookfield Park Primary School

The Playground

The playground is noisy,
The playground is loud.
You hear people screaming all around.
Balls bouncing in the air,
You see people doing their hair.

Helen Smith (9)
Brookfield Park Primary School

Playtime

The bell rings
The boys push
Girls shove.
Boys play football
We'll play basketball.
Girls natter
Boys patter.
Bell rings it's all over.

Lauren Kirk (9)
Brookfield Park Primary School

Playground

Playtime!
People screaming
Teachers shouting
Birds singing
Clock ticking
Bell ringing
Whistle blowing
Back to work
Again!

Bradley Gibson (9)
Brookfield Park Primary School

Playtime

Bell rings, playtime begins
Children rush,
Children push,
Out on the playground I make some new friends,
And play with my old friends too.

Daniel Hunt (8)
Brookfield Park Primary School

The Playground

It is fun on the playground
The children all run around.
When they're sad they run mild
When they're happy they run like a child.

Spencer Taylor-Williamson (10)
Brookfield Park Primary School

Playtimes

Playtime munchy
Packets of crisps crunchy
Kick a ball at the wall
'Time to go,' the teachers call.

Mollie Bloomfield (9)
Brookfield Park Primary School

Joy

Joy sounds like hummingbirds,
It looks like a beautiful rose.
Joy smells of fresh apple pie.
It feels like the softest silk.
Joy tastes of jelly and ice cream!
It lives in the mountains of wonderland.

Jessica Holt (9)
Chantlers Primary School

My Niece Is . . .

My niece is like an artist
She really likes art
Painting night and day
But she is not very smart.

Katrina Nicole (8)
Chantlers Primary School

Guilt

Guilt looks like a grey, dull day,
It feels like your heart is wrapped in tin foil
And smells like an old bottle of fiery smoke.
It sounds like the moan of insolent toddlers
And tastes like rotten, mouldy potatoes.
Guilt lives inside a corner of your stomach,
Only emerging when you've done something wrong.

Elizabeth Robson (9)
Chantlers Primary School

The Best Winter

W inter night frosty cold.
 I t is time to decorate the house.
N ow all the kids are being good
T he tree is up and decorated
E veryone is happy 'cause they got what they wanted
R iding on my sledge in the snow.

Liam Greer (9)
Chantlers Primary School

Happiness

Happiness smells like the lovely sweet perfume of roses.
It sounds like a piece of Beethoven's tremendous music
And feels as good as a brand, spanking new car.
It looks like a lovely bird ruffling its feathers in a large tree
But also tastes like a beautifully fresh apple.
Guess where it lives: deep inside my heart.

Tom Kay (9)
Chantlers Primary School

Happiness

Happiness sounds like a soft river flowing.
It smells like a syrup sweet
And feels as if a cute cat has been cuddled.
It looks like a fluffy teddy on a seat
Tastes like a sweet apple.
Happiness is everywhere if you look carefully.

Jack Hardman (10)
Chantlers Primary School

A Day In April

A day in April my sis saw
A *blue* kangaroo.
I think that day
Something strange was going on
At Chester Zoo,
I really do!

Lucy Spruce (10)
Chantlers Primary School

Fear

Fear sounds like the howling wind.
It looks pitch-black with shining teeth and wide eyes.
You can feel shivers ever so quickly running down the sharpest spine.
Fear smells like black, thick, choking smoke,
But tastes as vile as mouldy fruit,
And unfortunately, it belongs on this planet, floating around the sun.

Humira Fenn (9)
Chantlers Primary School

Promise

I	P	romise to
w	R	ite
m	O	re neatly
in	M	y classroom
	I	n my
	S	chool book
	E	very day!

Erin Middleton (10)
Chantlers Primary School

Promise

I	P	romise to
	R	ide
	O	n
	M	y
b	I	ke every
	S	unday of
	E	very week.

Charles Butterworth (9)
Chantlers Primary School

Promise

I	P	romise to
	R	ead
b	O	oks
	M	ore often
	I	n and out of
	S	chool
	E	very day!

Becci Byrne (9)
Chantlers Primary School

Promise

	P	romise to
I	R	emember
m	O	st
of	M	y
	I	mportant
	S	pellings
	E	very day.

Luke Collins (9)
Chantlers Primary School

Promise

	P	romise
I	R	ide
to	O	n
	M	y
b	I	ke
on	S	aturdays
nearly	E	very day.

Sam Hardacre (9)
Chantlers Primary School

Promise

	P	romise
I	R	owing with
to stop	O	lder sister
my	M	um and Dad
just for	I	don't get told off like
so	S	do
I alway	E	very single day and night.

Chloe Tomson (10)
Chantlers Primary School

Promise

I	P	romise to
stop	R	owing with my
y	O	unger sister
and help	M	y mum
	I	n the
hou	S	e for a
PS2 gam	E	I want.

Emma Dowd (10)
Chantlers Primary School

Promise

I	P	romise to
t	R	y
t	O	
	M	ake
	I	nformation
	S	ound
int	E	resting.

Chantelle Kennedy (9)
Chantlers Primary School

Promise

I	P	romise to
always	R	ead my home
reader b	O	ok by the end of
each	M	onth and
br	I	ng it
to	S	chool
	E	ach time.

Ashley Haggart (9)
Chantlers Primary School

I Promise

I P romise to
w R ite neatly
  O therwise
  M y mum
w I ll
  S hout
  E very day.

Tom Withers (9)
Chantlers Primary School

Winter

W ind is cold in winter,
 I cy cars can't start up so easily,
N ot a lot of children go out,
T urkey smells really nice,
E verybody plays with their new toys,
R ain and snow fall from the sky.

Richard Davies (8)
Chantlers Primary School

Anger

Anger sounds like nails scratching hard,
It smells of an acrid gas
And it feels like someone grabbing my heart.
It looks like a volcano erupting,
It tastes like car fumes.

Alexander McNicholas (9)
Chantlers Primary School

Anger

Anger sounds like a noisy beat
It looks like a fire meteor
It smells like an erupting volcano
And it feels as if someone's tightly gripping my heart.
It tastes like a sour lemon and it lives deep inside my mind.

Musa Khan (9)
Chantlers Primary School

My Friend

My friend is like a whirlwind,
She zooms past everything.
She could run round the world in a day
So fast she couldn't hear the school bell ring.

Taryn Mallison (9)
Chantlers Primary School

My Dad

My dad's like an expert at drawing,
He's better than me.
He wins all the competitions,
He is like the champion Tee!

Paige Owens (8)
Chantlers Primary School

My Brother Saw A Sleeping Panda

My brother saw a panda sleep,
On a July day in Beijing,
A hunter leapt and shot her, *bang!*
But he left her babies crying.

Sally Jones (10)
Chantlers Primary School

There Once Was a Young Man From Bury

There once was a young man from Bury
Who liked to eat lots of curry,
He once had a balti
Which was rather salty,
And that was the man from Bury.

Jake Howard (11)
Chantlers Primary School

There Was a Young Man Of Paris

There was a young man of Paris
Who said, 'I should live in a palace.'
He went to the king
And asked for a ring,
That silly young man of Paris.

Adam Fitton (11)
Chantlers Primary School

My Friend Is Like Beckham

My friend is like Beckham,
he bends it really good,
but when it comes to me,
I slip and fall in the mud.

Thomas Hopkinson (8)
Chantlers Primary School

My Sister's Like An Acrobat

My sister's like an acrobat,
She does loads more gym than me.
She can do bars, vault and floor,
And then come home for tea.

Lydia Stanton (8)
Chantlers Primary School

Jealousy

Jealousy lives in the darkest land,
On the darkest mountain
In the darkest cave.
I hear something howling,
I smell the worst,
It feels like it's scraping down my back
And looks like a demon illuminating the city below
It tastes like the sourest apple.
It slithers through the sewers and sneaks up to you.
Whenever you call for it,
It will come!

Ross Belch (9)
Chantlers Primary School

There Was An Old Man Named Terry

There was an old man named Terry
Who had a rather large belly,
He went to the gym,
But struggled to swim
And sank because of his belly.

Adam Hargreaves (11)
Chantlers Primary School

There Was Once A Boy From Darjeeling!

There was once a boy from Darjeeling
Who caught the express bus to Ealing,
The man near the door
Said, 'Don't sit on the floor,'
So he carefully sat on the ceiling.

Daniel Lewis (10)
Chantlers Primary School

The Gloomy Castle

The gloomy castle towered far above us into the darkness.
Bats swooped menacingly above our heads.
The old wooden gate creaked as we heaved it aside.
Graves engulfed the garden.
As we walked slowly past the graveyard,
We shivered as a chill wind swept round us.
As we opened the front door,
A metallic ringing sound echoed around us.
As we entered, we saw a spiral staircase
Twisting above our heads!
Many giant oil portraits hung on stone walls.
The whole house seemed to echo
With memories from the past,
Mostly bad ones . . .

Abigail Taylor-Spencer (9)
Chantlers Primary School

My Mum's Like A Machine

My mum's like a machine.
When we decide we are going to bake,
She already has the ingredients
And is halfway through the cake.

Katherine Burton (8)
Chantlers Primary School

My Poem

My friend is like a queen
and as pretty as a fairy.
She is very nice,
and not very scary.

Alana Grundy (9)
Chantlers Primary School

My Mum

My mum's like a librarian,
Because she loves to read.
She's always reading books,
It makes me feel like a seed.

Melissa Bailey (9)
Chantlers Primary School

My Poem

My brother's like a train,
he whistles all the time.
It's really sweet (but sometimes a pain)
and sometimes I wish it was a crime.

Rachel Moscrop (8)
Chantlers Primary School

My Sister

My sister's like Tim Henman,
Her ball goes right past my face.
She always beats my mum,
She is just an ace.

Rachel Flynn (8)
Chantlers Primary School

My Sister's Like A Gangster

My sister's like a gangster,
She raps better than me,
She pulls me by my ear,
And makes a cup of tea.

Victoria Newman (9)
Chantlers Primary School

Seasons

Spring
Spring is the time of year
When trees start to bloom.
A time to go outside,
So don't stay in your room.

Summer
Summer is a time of year
When leaves are on the trees.
You can go outside in the hot sun
And sometimes there's a breeze.

Autumn
Autumn is a time of year
When trees start to go bare.
There's carousels and other rides
At the funfair.

Winter
Winter is the time of year
When animals don't appear.
Yeah! Christmas is finally here!

Joseph Royle (9)
Chantlers Primary School

The Seasons

Winter brings the cold, cold sleet,
Snow and wind, frozen feet.

Spring brings little birds,
Sheep and cows in their herds.

Summer flowers like lilac and roses
All together make posies.

Autumn leaves drift to the floor,
Playing children shout for more.

Abigail Higham (9)
Chantlers Primary School

My Best Friend's Like A Fast Car

My best friend's like a fast car,
Racing straight past me.
He makes me look an idiot,
The fastest person I see.

Matthew Davis (9)
Chantlers Primary School

A Best Friend Is . . .

A best friend is someone that keeps all your secrets,
And when I close my eyes I can see the lovely memories,
I can see all the times we played nicely together
And all the happiness comes back again,
As if it was happening again.
They play with you when you are all on your own.
The memories are so nice that they are like
They are locked up in a prison.
A best friend is someone who is friendly and kind to you,
Forever, forever, forever!

Robyn Bailey (9)
Christ Church CE Walshaw Primary School

At Autumn Time

At autumn time, green leaves start to crunch up
And turn into brown, orange and gold.
At autumn time, the burning sun of summer
Starts to get freezing cold.
At autumn time, animals get ready for winter
And birds fly to hotter countries.
At autumn time, leaves are crowded in a pile on the floor.
At the end of autumn, it gets colder and is near to Christmas.
And then it is spring and it starts all over again.

Luke Benson (10)
Christ Church CE Walshaw Primary School

The Three Little Pigs

Once upon a time there were three little pigs.
Every night they each did a jig.
Their mum said, 'Move out, you are too old.
Don't worry about me, I won't be cold.'
So the first pig made his house of straw.
After a while, the wolf knocked at his door.
The wolf said, 'Let me come in,
Or I'll throw you in the stinky bin.'
The little pig shouted, 'No.'
So the horrible wolf began to blow.
The wolf gobbled up all the pork
And then he went for a long walk.
On his walk he came to a house
And he crept in as quiet as a mouse.
He saw a pig sitting on a chair,
The pig was eating a little pear.
The wolf ran over and started to eat,
So now he had had two helpings of meat.
'I am still not satisfied yet,
Another pig I will get.'
The wolf went to the house of bricks
And then started to do some high kicks.
He knocked the house down
And the pig did frown.
The pig got eaten
And the wolf said, 'I'll never be beaten.'

Lydia Instone (9)
Christ Church CE Walshaw Primary School

The Three Little Pigs

There once were three little pigs
Who lived with their mum, who fed them figs.
But one day their mother said, 'Out!'
So the pigs went away with what seemed to be nowt.
One little pig thought of making
His house of something by taking.
Meanwhile, the two little pigs
Kept on thinking till they thought
Of making their house of twigs.
Until one day, a boy called Darryl
Came with a machine gun
And hid behind a barrel.
Darryl went up to the house of twigs
And said, 'Little pigs, little pigs,
You're going to die unless you
Find a way of making me cry.'
So Darryl shot down the door
And killed the pigs,
And gave them to a wolf.

Darryl Owen (9)
Christ Church CE Walshaw Primary School

Explosions!

The people that really make me shiver
Are Miss Dynamite Pants and Captain Cod Liver.
They like the taste of crocodile bums,
Just to fill their bony tums!
Now Miss Dynamite Pants had one sly trick,
To blow up people's pants in just one tick!
There are three crocodiles
With big, juicy smiles,
But now those smiles have turned upside down,
Which makes a really big frown.
The crocs lived in three separate rivers,
And then appeared Miss D Pants and nine Cod Livers!

Madeleine McCann (10)
Christ Church CE Walshaw Primary School

The Three Little Pigs

Next to a river, by a wood,
Three little pigs, they all stood.
In the front room,
Mum said, 'Move or I'll boom.'
So they all moved out
Before they could shout.
So they all moved away.
The first pig did say,
'I'll build my house of straw,
You can build two more.'
Then the wolf came
And he was in fame.
He said, 'Little Pig, let me come in.'
But the pig was making an awful din
So he didn't hear the wolf at all,
Then the wolf started coming down the hall.
He found the pig in a room
And said, 'You're going to meet your doom.'
The wolf leapt on the pig,
He ate him and started doing a jig.
The wolf went looking for more pigs,
He found a house made out of twigs,
The sort a little pig would live in.
A pig is what the wolf would win.
Then the pig came trotting out,
Not knowing the wolf was about.
So he ate pig number two,
And he knew what to do.
He went to look for a third pig
And he saw a pig in a window doing a jig.
He went in and started eating him
And the light began to go dim.
The wolf said, 'I've had my fill,
And now I don't need my pill.'

Bethany Rawcliffe (9)
Christ Church CE Walshaw Primary School

The Three Little Pigs

Once upon a time, there were three pigs.
Their mum said, 'Get out of my home.'
The pigs said, 'Right then, we are going to live on our own.'
So the pigs set off and built a house of straw.
When they got in, a wolf came and said, 'I'll try not to break the law.'
The wolf went out and huffed and puffed.
The wolf blew the house down and he was quite chuffed.
Because the pigs had no house, they moved
To the other side of the forest and made a house of twigs.
They didn't want the wolf to come back,
So they dressed up and on their heads put hairy wigs.
The wolf knew they had dressed up and put wigs on their heads,
So he pegged them up with pencil leads,
And he went outside and huffed and puffed.
The wolf blew the house down and he was very chuffed.
The pigs moved near a building site and got some bricks and
                                           built a house.
The pigs didn't care if even in their house lived a mouse.
The wolf came back and huffed and puffed.
The wolf blew the house down and he was quite chuffed.
The wolf ate the three pigs and said, 'They taste quite good.'
For his dessert, he ate some mud.

Amber-Rose Perry (9)
Christ Church CE Walshaw Primary School

What Is A Ferrari?

A Ferrari is a speeding bullet going 250 miles an hour.
A Ferrari is a blazing red fire.
A Ferrari is a racing red cheetah.
A Ferrari is a shooting star in the sky.
A Ferrari is a racing shark in the sea.

Edmund Farrell (10)
Christ Church CE Walshaw Primary School

The Three Big Pigs

Once out in the Sahara Desert
There were three pigs who were quite pleasant.
But also there was a desert fox,
Who hated the smell of piggys' socks,
But because the smell was so, so strong,
It didn't take him very long
To sniff them out and track them down,
Although he always spat out their dressing gowns.
So soon he found two houses (of straw and of sticks)
And thought, *I'll blow them into bits!*
And so he blew and found right there
Two pigs in their underwear.
So he gobbled them up and of course
Spat out the gowns in his first course.
And then he found a house of bricks
And said, 'I'll blast it like those sticks.'
But he was not stupid and did not blow,
But instead got out a saxophone,
And played it so, so sad,
The bricks started crumbling rather bad.
So the pig inside quickly phoned
Miss Dyno-Knickers at her home.
So very soon she came along
And blew the fox up with some bombs,
That came straight from her knickers.
So the pig repaid her with some Snickers,
And they lived happily ever after,
The rest of their days filled with laughter.

Samantha Lees (10)
Christ Church CE Walshaw Primary School

A Best Friend Is . . .

A best friend is a person with whom I share happy memories,
When I look at photographs, it brings all the happy memories back.

A best friend is a fun person,
Like two kittens playing together kindly.

A best friend is a person who keeps secrets
Like they were locked away in a big box.

A best friend is a person who doesn't leave you out,
Like a pin out of its place.

A best friend is friendly,
Like part of your family.

A best friend is a person
Who likes what you do.

A best friend is really helpful,
Like a teacher.

Jessica Duckworth (9)
Christ Church CE Walshaw Primary School

What Is . . . A Star?

A star is a balloon
Shooting up in the sky.

A star is a racing car,
Zooming everywhere.

A star is a shark,
Bumping into everything.

A star is a coin
Falling down the grid.

A star is a piece of paper
Floating on top of the sea.

Hollie Vizard (10)
Christ Church CE Walshaw Primary School

Our World

Will there be
Clean air to breathe?
Will the streets be clean
When I grow up?

Will the grass still be green?
Will the sky still be blue?

Will we have fresh meat?
Will the fruit and vegetables be colourful?

Will there be colourful plants?
Will the trees still be green and give us oxygen?

Will the sea be clean?
Will the animals still be alive?

Will the people still be healthy
When I am all grown up?

Rebecca Sandford (9)
Christ Church CE Walshaw Primary School

What Is . . . A Lion?

A lion is a mass of orange and brown,
Splashed onto a white canvas.

A lion is a camouflaged predator
Ready to pounce.

A lion is a king of the jungle,
Who protects his family and land.

A lion is a pharaoh's pet,
Who protects his master.

A lion is a prowling animal
Never to be tamed.

Ashley Pickstone (10)
Christ Church CE Walshaw Primary School

On Our School Field

On our school field
Just yesterday,
A patterned wasp stung me,
Then flew away.

On our school field
I happened to hear
A police car wailing
In my ear.

On our school field
I smelt a flower,
The aroma was so lovely,
I stayed there for an hour.

On our school field
I noticed some footprints,
I decided to follow them,
So I took my mints.
(In case I got hungry.)

On our school field
I heard a bee
Buzzing in the flowers,
Freeeee!

On our school field
I smelt some grass,
Where a cat had dragged
Its breakfast; a bass.
(A type of fish.)

On our school field
I happened to see,
Its head in the clouds,
A big, tall tree.

On our school field
I heard a bird,
It was the sweetest tune
I had ever heard.

Megan Howard (10)
Christ Church CE Walshaw Primary School

At Autumn Time

At autumn time leaves start to fall
And sway gently to the ground.
They fall through the sky,
Like men working underground.

At autumn time, leaves turn into crust,
In mid-air they float through the sky.
The leaves change colour very quickly,
The trees are stood up very high.

At autumn time, squirrels gather food,
They hibernate in giant trees.
Their bodies are soft, fluffy and warm,
The wind is gentle like a breeze.

At autumn time the green leaves change colour,
The leaves go down like birds in the sky,
The birds migrate to warmer countries,
But only the ones who can fly.

At autumn time the leaves start to die,
The trees go darker every time.
The birds in the sky fly around,
So help the animals in that time.

David Stewart (10)
Christ Church CE Walshaw Primary School

What Is It Like?

Fumes are like an army of ghosts flying,
Oil is like a black monster seeking the fish,
Acid rain is concealed like a little bit of fire burning the plants,
Global warming is like a huge swimming pool drowning us all.
What will be left for me?

Ethan Turner (9)
Christ Church CE Walshaw Primary School

Autumn Time

The leaves change to red, orange and brown,
They drift down to the frozen ground.
The birds swoop as the days get shorter
And the nights get longer.

The squirrels collect their nuts
Then scurry off to hibernate.
The leaves all crunchy, like cereals for breakfast,
The bare trees all cold and shivery.

The summer clothes get put away
And out come jumpers,
Woolly pants, thick covers and night lamps.
The sky goes dull and days get darker.
Travelling gets harder and snow is coming.

Lucy Heys (9)
Christ Church CE Walshaw Primary School

On Our School Field

I can hear the big brown trees rustling in the wind.
On our school field I can hear birds singing beautiful songs,
Like the most tuneful flute.
On our school field I can hear Mr Webb's big, loud voice
Talking to everyone.
On our school field I can see football nets standing out
In the wind, big and strong.
On our school field I can see children playing kindly.
On our school field I can see the hill,
Big and green with the sweet smell of water.
On our school field I can smell the trees, the wind rustling.
On the school field I can smell the canteen,
Chips, beans and more.

Natasha Hamilton (10)
Christ Church CE Walshaw Primary School

Our Environment

Our environment
Is where we live.
If we destroy it,
Where will we live?

The animals are in great danger,
With all the rubbish on the floor,
Instead of the bin.

When you grow up
And look around,
What will you see?
Will you see fresh air and animals,
Or will you see rubbish?

All you've got to do to make a difference
Is just stop throwing rubbish,
And think about your future.

Amy Warner (9)
Christ Church CE Walshaw Primary School

My Future

Will you keep the water fresh?
Stop throwing fumes
And killing the fish.

Will you block the fumes in the cooling towers?
Stop adding fumes to the air,
Stop killing living things
And the acid rain
Killing flowers.

Stop throwing litter on the floor,
If glass was to be dropped,
Someone will be badly hurt.

Joshua Redgrave (9)
Christ Church CE Walshaw Primary School

What Will There Be Left For Me?

What will be left
Of the world
When I grow up?

Have you used all
The fresh air?
Will there be any
Left for me?

Will the world
Be green and beautiful,
Or will it be
Black and horrid?

Will there be
Oxygen from the trees?
Will we survive?

Will there be
Fruit from the trees,
Or will all of them die?

Lucy Allen-Baines (8)
Christ Church CE Walshaw Primary School

What Will It Be Worth?

What will it be worth if you have used the goodness up?

What will it be worth?
What will it be worth?

What will it be worth if we destroy the world?

What will it be worth?
What will it be worth?

What will it be worth if we destroy the animals?
What will it be worth if we destroy the world?
What will it be worth if we kill Mother Nature?

Jonathon Berry (9)
Christ Church CE Walshaw Primary School

What Will Earth Be Like?

When I grow up,
Will the air be clean?

Will the noise be calm?
Will plants grow?

When I grow up,
Will the water be clean?
Will there be fish left in the sea?

When I grow up,
Will the lights be calm?
Will the floor be clean?

When I grow up,
Will the noise be quiet?
Will the people survive?

When I grow up,
Will the Earth be clean?

When I grow up,
Will it be a happy Earth?

Lisa McDermott (8)
Christ Church CE Walshaw Primary School

My Future

Will there be any plants?
Will there be any farms?
Will I ever grow up?
Will you keep the water clean?
Will there be any animals left?

When I grow up, the world will be beautiful.

Remesha Sutherland (8)
Christ Church CE Walshaw Primary School

Stop That Pollution!

Pollution is really, really bad,
It makes the wildlife very sad.
What will be left for me?

Will oil cover the sea?
Will there be a beautiful scent,
Or will there be a nasty scent?

Will you spill chemicals,
Or will you make sure
Chemicals don't ruin the floor?

Will fish die out?
Will animals become extinct,
Or will you make sure they are safe?

Now you make sure
Everything is safe,
So pollution doesn't happen anymore!

Sian Devine (8)
Christ Church CE Walshaw Primary School

No Air To Breathe

Will there be
No acid rain,
But clean rain
Instead?

Will there be
Animals to see
And to feed?

Will the plants
Still give
Us oxygen to breathe?
What will be my future?

Rachel Taylor (8)
Christ Church CE Walshaw Primary School

My Future

What will there be?
Will there be whales with their very long tails?
Will there be fish in the sea?
Will there be a moon and a sun,
And will there be anything for me?

Will the sky be blue?
Will the grass be green?
Will the sun be bright,
And will there be anything for me?

Will there still be spring, summer, autumn and winter?
Will we still have a king or a queen?
Will there be anything left for us
And will there be anything for me?

Lara Sugden (8)
Christ Church CE Walshaw Primary School

Stop Pollution

Pollution is an
Animal killer,
Chaos bringer,
Air stealer . . .
Pollution,
Pollution.

Pollution is a
Chemical mixer,
Trouble maker,
Water poisoner,
So stop pollution!

Ashley Brooks (8)
Christ Church CE Walshaw Primary School

My Future

Will there be
Pure air to breathe?
Will the rivers and sea be clean?

Will the animals
Be alive, so we
Can have food?

Will trees
Still be green?
Will we still have paper to write on?

Will we still
Have cars?
Will we have to ride horses?

Will blue whales sing?
Will elephants
And rhino still survive?

Will you have left
Us anything
Healthy and alive?

Jonathan Barnes (8)
Christ Church CE Walshaw Primary School

The Future

Will we have animals, coals or gases?
If we do, we won't have masses.

Will I have my life,
To carve things with a knife,
Or will the world be gone?

When I'm up there,
Will there be safe air,
Or people to love and care?

Joshua Brownlow (9)
Christ Church CE Walshaw Primary School

My Future

Will there
Be anything
Left when
I'm older?

Will there
Be mountains,
Tall and proud?
Will there be a
Blue sea?

Will tarmac
Cover the
Fresh, green
Grass?

Will pollution
Kill fish and
Destroy the
Rivers?

Will toxic fumes
Kill birds?
Will they poison
Clean air?

James Dutka (8)
Christ Church CE Walshaw Primary School

My Future

What do you smell?
Fresh air?
It is a sign of breathing.
Car fumes polluting.
What do you see?
Another thing you
Don't see is sewage.
Don't smoke or make noises.

Mylo Dougherty (8)
Christ Church CE Walshaw Primary School

Pollution Kennings

Poison thrower,
Oxygen taker,
Animal killer,
Litter dropper,
Tree dyer,
Dirty river,
Fire leaper,
Smoke bringer,
Car fume,
Bird shouter,
Fish poisoner,
Dark sky bringer,

Pollution!

Ailisha Cooper (8)
Christ Church CE Walshaw Primary School

My Future

When I grow up, the air might be polluted.
The rivers might be full of rubbish.
The hot beaches might be full of rubbish.
The acid rain might kill the flowers.
Will the sky still be blue?
Will the grass still be green?

Ross Allen (8)
Christ Church CE Walshaw Primary School

Kawasaki

I have a motorbike, it's a Kawasaki,
When I ride it's really fast!
When I race I'm never last!
Some people say it's rather tacky,
But I think it's really wacky!

Joe Geeling (10)
Guardian Angels' RC Primary School

Darkness

Darkness is black like a
Freezing, frosty night.
It sounds like someone screaming
From being in a cold, icy prison.
It tastes like bitter blood swimming
Around in my mouth.

It smells like a burning fire,
Coming from a dark and cool forest.
It looks like someone being killed
In the middle of the night.

It feels like holding sharp, sticky
Branches of a tree in your hand.
It reminds me of watching a scary movie
At the dead of night.

Victoria McCauley (11)
Guardian Angels' RC Primary School

Night

Night is gloomy with shadows,
People are creepy and still
And the creatures are crawling
And eyes are peering through bushes.

As the river flows gently,
The trees are swaying,
Cats are pouncing and purring,
Lamp posts are swinging and screeching.

Weird shadows appearing on the golden grass,
Thick, black stillness from the trees.
Bats and owls staring from up above,
Stars glittering in the black sky.

Dominic Anderson (11)
Guardian Angels' RC Primary School

Night

London station never seemed so quiet,
The café sign swinging, screeching,
Looking up into the night,
The thick, black stillness enfolding around me.

Creatures watching, eyes peering,
Cats prowling, bats shuddering.
I back away slowly, but hit the wall,
They close in on me, I fall.
Their nefarious plan does not work,
I creep to the door and give it a kick.

The bats are too quick, they quiver over the door,
I run out fast, all the animals disappear.
Sit on a creaky bench, waiting,
The track shaking, my heart pounding.

Suddenly a huge steam train there before me,
All doors open.
Above the door, on a dusty plate says,
'Come on board, if you dare!'

Sophie Balmbra (10)
Guardian Angels' RC Primary School

Night

Darkness deepens in the night,
Daylight lost and vanished in the dark,
The atmosphere is gathering around,
Leaves are shivering, making a petrifying sound.

Shadows are emerging from out of sight,
Shivers are approaching behind.
Creatures glare up at you,
Restless shadows just don't give up.

Darkness is fading into the light,
Darkness is going now,
But it will be back.

Natasia Coote (10)
Guardian Angels' RC Primary School

Night

Outside is full of darkness,
Trees move their arms slowly.
Owls hoot in the misty breeze.
Black, creeping shadows move across the alleyway,
Street lights flicker, as they are just about to go out.

Outside is full of mysterious movement.
Eyes peer as if they are ready to pounce on you,
Squirrels creep as quietly as mice through leaves,
To find a place for the night.

Outside is full of noises,
Bats screech as they talk to one another,
Burglar alarms beep as someone sets them off.

Outside is full of darkness.

Rebecca Hajdukewycz (11)
Guardian Angels' RC Primary School

Love

Love is the colour pink, the heart of
Valentine's Day passed to everyone.
It feels like the lovely hug from a cuddly bear
On a cold winter's day.
It smells like the beautiful scent of a rose
Bursting out of the ground.
It looks like a bunny rabbit leaping around,
Just learned to run.
It sounds like a little newborn baby's first cry.
It tastes like a delicious chocolate bar
Melting at the back of your throat.
It reminds me of a giant cloud floating overhead,
With its brilliant dreams placing love in our hearts.

Lauren Doughty (11)
Guardian Angels' RC Primary School

Fear

Fear is as black as the cold night's air,
Creeping up on you when you don't know it's there.

It sounds like the eerie owl's hoot,
The rustle of leaves, the stomp of a boot.

It tastes like branches stabbing at your throat,
It tastes like waves crashing at your boat.

It smells like a steaming hot kettle,
When your hand sticks to the metal.

Fear looks like a sly glare,
It looks horrid, too horrid to bear.

It feels like a hard, harsh slap,
When the mysterious wind gives you a tap.

Fear reminds me of a weeping child,
A huge garden, creepy and wild.

Beth Banim (10)
Guardian Angels' RC Primary School

Night

Darkness creeps all around me,
Graveyards looking bare,
Trees' arms reaching out to grab me
To carry me in mid-air.
The wind is howling,
The bats are swooping.

Creatures lurching in the pitch-black,
Sound there is none here,
Feels like every step I take is being watched.
The wind is howling,
The bats are swooping.

Rebecca Cooper (11)
Guardian Angels' RC Primary School

Night

A crooked house waving in the wind
The ghosts of people who have not sinned
The creek of floorboards,
The screech of doors.

A crooked house waving in the wind,
It shows people who have been pinned,
Things scattering,
Pipes rattling.

A crooked house waving in the wind,
Rolling around, things that have not been binned,
The darkness of the night,
It's better when it's bright.

Charlotte McDonald (11)
Guardian Angels' RC Primary School

The Silent Killer!

The panther silent as it lurks in the grass.
Unseeable as its sleek, black fur hides its presence from the prey.
Silent, while it elegantly stalks its prey.
Deadly with its razor sharp claws and teeth, ready to kill.
Cunning as it waits for the precise moment to attack.
Unforgiving as it sinks its magnificent teeth into the flesh of a deer.
Ferocious and powerful with the taste of blood, nothing can stop it.

Alexander Hall (11)
Guardian Angels' RC Primary School

The Cheetah

Cheetahs are as fast as cars,
Running wildly and free searching for food,
As quickly as possible racing home to his family,
To see his children protecting them from humans,
So they don't have to live behind bars.

Adam Mortimer (11)
Guardian Angels' RC Primary School

I've Heard Your Cries

I've heard your cries, my beautiful stallion,
Taken from your home so suddenly,
Into a world of wickedness and slavery.
Into a world you've never seen before,
Into a world where faces are dark and poisoned.
So different,
From the peaceful home you love.

I've heard your cries, my beautiful stallion,
No more running freely on the grass so green,
With your coat so black glimmering in the sun.
I feel your eyes ablaze with anger,
For being taken from the wild,
I know what you wish,
To be free once more, my beautiful stallion.

Joanna Rector (10)
Guardian Angels' RC Primary School

Goldfish

Roll up! Roll up!
See the goldfish in his tank.
Swimming around quite boring,
Living a goldfish life.
See this orange creature,
Although they call him Gold.
Forever blowing bubbles
In the same old bowl.
How he wishes to be free,
Dreaming of a life in the deep blue sea.
But then again he's better off
In his small old tank,
He's just another goldfish
Living a pointless life.

Sean Farrelly (11)
Guardian Angels' RC Primary School

Silence

Silence is as white as snow,
It sounds like a peaceful summer's day,
It tastes like a sweet piece of cake,
It smells like lavender-scented bubble bath,
It looks like a calm, loving angel
Floating above your head,
It feels like a soft woolly jumper
Rubbing against your neck,
It reminds me of when I go to bed.

Rebecca Leveridge (11)
Guardian Angels' RC Primary School

Darkness

Darkness is black like a starry night,
It sounds like a danger threat.
It tastes like treacle toffee in a bowl,
It smells like a burning fire in the woods,
It looks like a raging bull in the dark,
It feels like a thrilling feeling in the forest,
It reminds me of being in my bed with no light on.

Aidan Robinson (10)
Guardian Angels' RC Primary School

My Favourite Animal

Guinea pigs soft, furry and brown,
Nice and cuddly all year round.
Their eyes gleam like the warm sun,
Chewing on their food,
That's their idea of fun!
Their fur being slowly, softly brushed,
When I clean away all last year's dust.
Their ears so tiny, cute and small,
But they can still hear my soft, gentle call.

Jessica Millington (10)
Guardian Angels' RC Primary School

Night

Floorboards creaking
Shadows bouncing off every wall
Clock ticking
Time going really slowly
Can't sleep
Things running through my mind
Worrying about the next day.

Bats flapping
Dogs howling
Imagination exploding
The sparkling tap dripping
Doors opening from the strong wind outside.

Pictures' eyes watching you
As you go around the house
Curtains opening and closing,
This is why I'm scared of the *night!*

Emily Richards (11)
Guardian Angels' RC Primary School

Spooky

Outside is an old house,
Outside the old house is a spooky tree,
On the spooky tree are two yellow eyes,
Outside the spooky tree is a creepy shadow
Moving towards the house,
Inside the spooky house is a creaky staircase,
Up the spooky staircase is a mouse scuttling for food,
Around the spooky corner in a room,
Inside the spooky room are two coffins,
Inside the old coffins,
Are bugs, eating the flesh off the bodies,
Outside the death room is another room,
Inside that room *boo* is me.

Scott Sweatman (11)
Guardian Angels' RC Primary School

Mummy

Mummy's the first word I learnt to say,
She loves me deeply in every way.

Each minute she's always rich with care,
Even though she's starting with grey hair.

But looks don't matter, it's the heart-warming part,
She's told me many times that I'm her sweetheart.

She saves me spicy ribs to eat,
And gives me the ones full of meat.

She used to make me happy,
Whilst changing my nappy.

She taught me not to suck my thumb
That's why I love my mum!

Naomi Ritchie (10)
Guardian Angels' RC Primary School

Night

Shadow on the wall, seldom a word,
Never mind that noise you heard,
It's just the beasts under your bed,
Behind your curtains, in your head.

The door is locked, but opens still,
The creak of floorboards soft, but shrill,
Sweat is dripping off your head,
Lying still, inside your bed.

The wind outside whips the trees,
Through the window creeps a shivering breeze,
It's just the beasts under your bed,
Behind your curtains, in your head.

Adam Warburton (11)
Guardian Angels' RC Primary School

Creeping Shadows

Shadows creeping slyly,
Outside my bedroom door,
Figures stealing, eyes creeping,
Something's gone on tour.

The curtains to my window are
Dark, ragged and poor,
And the switch to my light
Is very insecure.

Shadows creeping slyly,
Outside a creaking door,
The arms of a glowing tree,
The running of a wolf,
Searching for its tea!

Christie Stefaniuk (11)
Guardian Angels' RC Primary School

Brothers

Brothers are sweet
And can be a treat.

Brothers are cute,
They always put on your boot.

Brothers are annoying,
But you do adore them.

Some people don't want any,
But some people do,
I'll soon have two!

Samantha Williams (11)
Guardian Angels' RC Primary School

Shopping

Lipstick, denim skirts, all those shoes,
High heels, trainers you cannot choose.
Ponchos, PJs, underwear and more,
All those items - clothes galore.

Hair clips, hair bands, stuff that rule,
Don't listen to anyone - shopping is cool!
Jackets, coats, party dresses too,
Miss a shopping sale, you had better not do.

Designers, stilettos and leather belts,
Earrings, necklaces, fabrics and felts,
Cotton, silk, cashmere and tweeds,
Shopping is what a young girl needs!

Alexandria Eleanor Willan (11)
Guardian Angels' RC Primary School

Night

No people in sight, the tension is building,
It's all quiet apart from the spine-chilling
Screeching from the bats,
Goblins crawling around you as you shake with fear,
Horrible sounds from the forest floor as creepy
Crawlies scurry around,
Then a sound of a bat with a deafening screech.

Terrifying trouble feeling close to you,
It's too spooky to escape from a real life nightmare,
My instincts are telling me to hide,
Eaten up by fright inside my mind.

John Walsh (11)
Guardian Angels' RC Primary School

Peace

The moon shines down turning everything to silver
The lake reflects, the moons beams.
The cats on the roof look down on the slumbering village,
Their eyes reflecting the moon's light,
The people dreaming glorious dreams,
The whole night is calm - nothing has stirred,
The world has stopped, it is all calm,
The whole world is peaceful.

Nathan Plumridge (10)
Guardian Angels' RC Primary School

My Bedroom

Pink and yellow is my room,
Right next to the loo,
Busted plays along the track,
Cool! Cool! Cool!
My Nintendo makes a loud, loud noise,
As it tracks along the games,
Come to my room and hear the noise,
Come on, you need to come!

Amy Pagan (7)
Heskin Pemberton CE Primary School

My Bedroom

My room is pink and blue,
So cool for a pretty, pink sleeping bag,
My mum thinks my bedroom is so cool,
For pretty pink make-up,
I have a lot of colourful clothes,
To have a fashion show.

Lucy Roocroft (8)
Heskin Pemberton CE Primary School

My Club House

Up the side lovely ladders
Get climbed on with shudders.
Girlie games makes
Me go insane.
Perfect paintings, gosh!
My family's fainting.

How do you do?
I think you're pretty cool!
Proper paint, pretty paint
Why I can't wait?
Cool carpet on the floor
Things are coming from the door.

Cheeky charms, beady bracelets,
Nancy note pads on all
The dazzling desks,
Everything is tidy, not a mess.

Brilliant balcony all around the house,
Little squeaking like a miniature mouse.
Who's that creeping behind the door?
Look it's my fantastic friends,
The party's time to end.

Gabrielle Stringfellow (8)
Heskin Pemberton CE Primary School

My Bedroom

My bedroom has a broken, blue chair
And in it sits a ripped teddy bear.
Half-cut curtains and an old wooden stool
And a very, very small swimming pool.
There is lots of clutter on the floor
And everyday it piles up more and more.
Lots of loud sounds as the radio pounds
And lots of loud noise from the girls and boys.

Bethany Patton, Megan Price & Natasha Croager (7)
Heskin Pemberton CE Primary School

The Stables

When you can smell that horsey smell
You feel like going in further,
Sniffing and whiffing, what can you smell?
That golden sand paddock, horses trotting round.
There's my best horse stamping on the ground.
Each step I take I smell something different,
Carrots crunching in horses' mouths,
Polos dropping.
As I step I smell something different,
The clenching reins
And a messy storeroom.
I see a horse that needs a groom.
As I pick up the prickly brush
The horse rubs me on the nose.
I stop,
My mum is calling,
'It is time to go.'

Tabatha Lamb (8)
Heskin Pemberton CE Primary School

My Hotel

You walk into a red reception,
Posher than you see on television,
Smart ladies stand behind dazzling desks,
There isn't a single bit of mess.

Follow the signs to the bar,
What can you see?
Ladies and children drinking lemonade
And men drinking beer.

Smart ladies walking upstairs,
Start the holiday with no cares,
Unpack their case, tie their shoelace,
We hope they have a lovely day.

Amy Murphy (7)
Heskin Pemberton CE Primary School

My Living Room

My silver TV standing very still,
The fire lit, that's cosy and warm,
Sofa so comfy,
Shiny DVD that spins round,
Delicate ornaments standing on the shelf,
Crystals sparkling in the light,
The rug so colourful,
The carpet so golden,
This is my favourite place in the night.

Emma Hazeldine (9)
Heskin Pemberton CE Primary School

My Bedroom

My bedroom is my private room,
Full of my special things,
My grandad's old fashioned cars stand out
And so does my black guitar.
My PlayStation and my black television,
Stands on my shelf,
My stereo sits on a separate shelf,
Next to my skateboarding bed.

Jack Sumner (8)
Heskin Pemberton CE Primary School

My Special Place

My room is as tidy as the Queen's room,
Clothes in wardrobes, toys in tubs
And make-up in a silver box.
Yellow moon rocker rocks through mid-air,
My dazzling desk shines up and over,
Maybe even down.
I love my room,
I want to stay and rest all day.

Bethany Cooper (9)
Heskin Pemberton CE Primary School

My Room

Come into my room,
It won't be your doom,
I hate girls
And like boys
And have lots of toys,
My room is cool,
But I don't like school.
Check out my PS2,
People like it, but do you?
I hear sheep as I peep
Through the door,
That's all, that's cool,
Sorry there's no more.

James Forshaw (8)
Heskin Pemberton CE Primary School

My Bedroom

My bedroom
Is a moon
It glows all through
The night.
Cuddly teddies everywhere,
I love my teddies,
I hug them tight.

Magical make-up on
Dazzling desks,
Nobody's making such a mess.

Eleanor Gray (7)
Heskin Pemberton CE Primary School

My Bedroom

My room is blue,
Right next to the loo,
With the ongoing PS2,
There's mess in there too,
So come in and
It will be the end of you!

Under the bed are lots of toys,
Old PS1s and Game Boys,
Are all forgotten toys
And they all belong to us . . .
Boys!

Jack Wright (9)
Heskin Pemberton CE Primary School

My Bedroom

My bedroom is full of space,
But it's very good fun,
Best of all I like my books
And the fun board games.
Lots of teddies I have got
Sitting in a big floppy net.
A bed as tall as an elephant
And a ladder to climb up its back,
Underneath is a tent to hide from my sister,
My bedroom is full of fun.

Freddie Hughes (8)
Heskin Pemberton CE Primary School

Our Bedroom

Our bedroom is all Man U,
Mess it up and you'll get sued,
Silver TVs, PlayStation too,
If you touch it,
Goodbye to you!

Lots of CDs and DVDs,
Under the bed, pretend guns and cars,
On the PS2, lots of toys, fizzy Coke too,
End of the day goodnight to you.

Cameron Jeffers & Jack Clarke (8)
Heskin Pemberton CE Primary School

My Bedroom

In my room is a silvery black TV,
I like watching funny cartoons,
My PlayStation is silver,
I like games too.

In my room is a wobbly bed,
Lots of toys too,
If you touch the PS2, don't!
We're warning you.

Jimmy Wright (7) & Josh Johnson (8)
Heskin Pemberton CE Primary School

My Dog . . .

My dog is as giddy as a clown,
As she runs around the field,
Chase her, but you can't keep up,
She protects me like a shield.

Matthew Hook (10)
Highfield St Matthew's CE Primary School

Stacey Sinclair

My name is Stacey Sinclair
And I like to brush my hair,
My best friend's Lauren Lindly
And she wants to live in Hindly,
I love to dance and while I prance,
I have two pet fish and I'm getting a dog, I wish!

Stacey Sinclair (9)
Highfield St Matthew's CE Primary School

Scoring

Scoring, scoring,
It is fine,
One day soon,
That goal's mine,
When I make that goal mine,
I'm the best scorer of all time.

Jamie Lindley (10)
Highfield St Matthew's CE Primary School

Pineapple - Haiku

Your skin is prickly,
You have a very good hair-do
And your skin is brown.

Joshua Parker (9)
Highfield St Matthew's CE Primary School

Plum

Plum, you are sweet
Purple and juicy
And soft just to chew.

Lewis Wright (9)
Highfield St Matthew's CE Primary School

School Life

I started school at the age of four,
I felt quite scared like never before,
Then Mrs Carter I did see
And with a smile she welcomed me.

Now I'm five, no longer four,
Into Year 1 with Ms Moore,
She asked my mum to help us bake,
So in she came to bake a cake.

Mrs Cavanagh I had in Year 2,
A part in the nativity we had to do,
I got butterflies on the day,
Stood in church narrating a play.

We had Mrs Hayes in Year 3,
Her fashion really did impress me,
Purple boots she wore on her feet,
Being in Year 3 was really neat.

I loved to read in Year 4,
But Mrs Layland taught me to love it more,
Many books she lent to me,
That's what made us so happy.

In Year 5 Mr Broadstock we had,
He made us all happy when we were sad,
I'm useless at sport, that's right, *them all*!
But the bad thing was he was good at football.

Mrs Holcroft is helping us now,
I want to look forward to SATs but *how*?
At the end of the year, we're doing our play,
Time at school has gone like a day.

My future now is High School,
That lies ahead of me,
I think it will be quite hard,
But we'll just have to wait and see.

Amy Stringman (11)
Highfield St Matthew's CE Primary School

Timmy Dilver

Timmy Dilver comes to stay,
With eyes as gleaming as a sunny day,
Ears like shells and teeth like silver,
A bash of a boy, is Timmy Dilver.

His tummy is round and his neck is a frown
And all of his hair is nearly put down,
His clothes are enough to attract no shark
And on his trousers is left no mark.

Daniel Stringman (8)
Highfield St Matthew's CE Primary School

Youth And Old Age

Youth is like a person full of joy,
Age is a nightmare,
Youth is like a spring day,
Age is like a bad dream.

Youth is like a warm summer's day,
Age is like a spooky house,
Youth is great, age is scary,
Youth is bright and sunny.

Jade Nolan (11)
Highfield St Matthew's CE Primary School

Diamond Spinner

A sculpture of nature,
Right before my eyes,
Glistening, shining in the golden light,
Like a lace of diamonds,
Threaded in fascinating spirals,
Made by nature's greatest artist,
Mother spider.

Molly Selby (11)
Highfield St Matthew's CE Primary School

Sea Scene

A gust of wind blowing through the sea,
One young sea diver swimming with the fish,
Two toddlers catching the wild waves,
A boat bobbing and crashing around the sea,
Seven starfishes dilly dancing in the sea,
A tin can floating far out at sea,
Eleven octopuses dancing on their legs,
Two children swimming slowly back to shore,
A woman far out at sea just lying on a lilo
And a baby learning to swim.

Melissa Jones (8)
Highfield St Matthew's CE Primary School

Prison

Walls of iron, walls of steel,
Guards all around the walls of prison,
Watching every move you make,
Until you're locked up at night in the dark,
People wailing and groaning,
Until that day,
When you're released into civilisation.

James McHugh (10)
Highfield St Matthew's CE Primary School

Night Poem

Night comes with trees whistling,
Night comes with the sky hissing,
Night comes with people talking,
Night comes with people walking,
Night comes with cars cruising,
Night is a nurse that puts you to sleep.

David Griffiths-Naylor (9)
Highfield St Matthew's CE Primary School

Football Poem

A midfielder, defender, goalie, striker
Are all in a football team.
The team will make us super proud,
So shout it, scream it, sing it loud.
Hear the songs from the Anfield crowd,
Benitez shouting at the side,
A midfield pass on the wide,
Bring it to the wing, cross it high,
To the striker head it . . .

A fantastic goal from Morientes
Passed from Louis Garcia,
The crowd arise with open eyes
To see the ball in the back of the net!
What a surprise.

Jade Cartwright (11)
Highfield St Matthew's CE Primary School

Sea Scene

A bunch of people playing ball,
Two toddlers splashing joyfully,
Seven people happily sitting in a boat,
Six people skiing on the water,
A group of starfish sticking to the seabed,
Three seagulls hunting for food,
Nine people making waves in the sea,
Four people swimming proudly,
Five groups of people going on a boat trip,
Eight young children dancing in the water,
One toddler singing in the sea
And a child sitting down in the water.

Alexandra Jo Clark (8)
Highfield St Matthew's CE Primary School

Night Comes

Night comes
With my brother snoring.

Night comes
With mums and dads shouting.

Night comes
With a hedgehog rustling.

Night comes
With a golden tree swirling.

Night comes
With the hot sun hiding.

Night comes
With lightning flashing.

Andrew Saxon (8)
Highfield St Matthew's CE Primary School

Night-Time Comes

Night-time comes,
With teenagers shouting.

Night-time comes,
With ajar doors shutting.

Night-time comes,
With a baby screaming.

Night-time comes,
With a TV talking.

Night-time comes,
With a beer can clinking.

Night-time comes,
With a grey wolf howling.

Sean Hewitt (8)
Highfield St Matthew's CE Primary School

Evening

Evening comes,
With Dad's snoring.

Evening comes,
With trees blowing.

Evening comes,
With bats flapping.

Evening comes,
With owls swooping.

Evening comes,
With noises.

Evening comes,
With mice scattering.

Evening comes,
With skunks smelling.

Evening comes,
With adults laughing.

Evening comes with
Carrying me to bed.

Lauren Melling (8)
Highfield St Matthew's CE Primary School

Sea Scene

One little boat gently tossing on the waves,
Children playing in the sea,
Dolphins diving to and fro,
Fish swimming here and there,
A beach ball floating everywhere,
A seagull hunting for his food,
A bunch of seaweed floating by.

Sophie Brown (8)
Highfield St Matthew's CE Primary School

Sally Rivers

Sally Rivers comes to stay,
You can tell she came to play,
Her hair is black and long,
And while she's at it, she always sings a song.

Sally Rivers likes to play tennis all day,
Anywhere in any sort of way,
She likes to take a walk down the street
And while she's at it, she shuffles her feet.

Sally Rivers always goes to the swimming pool
And Sally says she's always very cool,
Now it's the weekend,
Sally has made a new friend.

Her clothes are squeaky clean
And she's never ever mean,
Sally's teeth are as white as a paper sheet
And she likes to drink fizzy pop in the heat.

Sally is an angel for her mum and dad,
They say she is the best girl they've ever had,
Sally knows how to speak French
And while she does it, she sits on the bench.

Kayleigh Anderson (9)
Highfield St Matthew's CE Primary School

Sea Fun

A lilo floating on the sea,
Two children playing,
Two ducks underwater,
Two grandparents lying in the shade,
Three dads boogying to their head sets,
Six mums getting brown in the sun,
Twelve speedboats going fast on the sea.

Leah Coates (9)
Highfield St Matthew's CE Primary School

Windy Nights

Whenever the moon and stars are set,
Whenever the wind is high,
All night long in the dark and wet,
A man goes riding by,
Late in the night when the fires are out,
Why does he gallop and gallop about?

Whenever the trees are crying out loud,
And the ships are tossed at sea,
By one the highway, low and proud,
By at the gallop goes he,
By at the gallop he goes, and then,
By he comes back at the gallop again.

Sophie Atherton (9)
Highfield St Matthew's CE Primary School

Night

Night comes with cats miaowing,
Night comes with babies,
Night comes with dads groaning,
Night comes with dogs barking,
Night comes with people snoring,
Night comes with telephones ringing.

Thomas Wheeler (8)
Highfield St Matthew's CE Primary School

Night

Night comes with big sisters talking,
Night comes with people snoring,
Night comes with telephones ringing.

Abbie Whelan (9)
Highfield St Matthew's CE Primary School

Night-Time

Night-time comes,
With Mum and Dad shouting.

Night-time comes,
With a hedgehog sniffling.

Night-time comes,
With a dustbin rattling.

Night-time comes,
With a TV booming.

Night-time comes,
With a cat miaowing.

Night-time comes,
With the carpet creaking.

Jack Macdonald (9)
Highfield St Matthew's CE Primary School

Night

Night comes,
With a hedgehog scrunching.

Night comes,
With lightning flashing.

Night comes,
With loud winds howling.

Night comes,
With dustbins rattling.

Night comes,
With big trees swaying.

Night comes,
With bright stars shining.

Daniel McNamara (8)
Highfield St Matthew's CE Primary School

Night Comes

Night comes
With winds whistling.

Night comes
With green trees swishing.

Night comes
With werewolves howling.

Night comes
With hunters hunting.

Night comes
With thunder crashing.

Night comes
With owls twitching.

Liam Heaton (8)
Highfield St Matthew's CE Primary School

Spider - Haiku

The shiny web glows
With blinding silver sunlight
The spider curled up.

Matthew Price (8)
Highfield St Matthew's CE Primary School

Grapes - Haiku

You grow on thin vines,
You are small, green and juicy,
You are lovely grapes.

Amy Barlow (8)
Highfield St Matthew's CE Primary School

Night Comes

Night comes with cars passing,
Night comes with dogs barking,
Night comes with trucks beeping,
Night comes with my mum singing,
Night comes with wind swishing,
Night comes to tuck me into bed.

Archie Selby (8)
Highfield St Matthew's CE Primary School

Apple - Haiku

Apple you are green,
Apple you are delicious,
Apple you are sweet.

Joshua Steven Gannon (8)
Highfield St Matthew's CE Primary School

Banana - Haiku

You are yellow and
You are like a boomerang,
Mmm you are juicy.

Cara Aston (8)
Highfield St Matthew's CE Primary School

Night

Darkness is here now,
As the bright moon shines up high,
Everything is still.

Alexandra Rayner (9)
Highfield St Matthew's CE Primary School

School Days

School is sometimes boring,
School is sometimes crazy,
The children like to giggle,
Sometimes it is weird
And sometimes it is cool,
But all the time children rule.

Janet Waterworth (9)
Highfield St Matthew's CE Primary School

Night Sky - Haiku

Darkness is now still
Jewels illuminate the dark
Tiny lights fly by.

Samantha Brown (9)
Highfield St Matthew's CE Primary School

Pear

You are mouth-watering,
You are brown and yellow and sweet,
You are really juicy.

Jamie Carney (8)
Highfield St Matthew's CE Primary School

The Rainbow Man - Haiku

The rainbow man stands
Reaching up high for the clouds
Colours gleaming bright.

Jason Williams (9)
Highfield St Matthew's CE Primary School

Dinner Time Queue

It's bangers and mash my little ones,
Not spaghetti or soup, line up, don't push,
It's not polite, it's rude.

I'm hungry, I'm starving,
I want my lunch, I've worked very hard
All day, he's got in cos he's pushed in
And it's not fair.
Be quiet, don't shout, you'll soon be served,
There's plenty of good in the pot,
If you behave there's seconds to come
So give it your best shot.

Oh please, oh please give us a clue
And I'll show you what I can do.

Aaron Sibblies (11)
Highfield St Matthew's CE Primary School

Dinner Time Queue

It's bangers and mash, my little ones, not spaghetti or
Soup, line up, don't push, I've told you before, it's not
Polite, it's rude.

I'm hungry, I'm starving, I want my lunch,
I've worked very hard all day,
He's got his cos he's pushed in and it's not fair!
Be quiet, don't shout, you'll soon be served,
There's plenty of food in the pot,
If you behave there's seconds to come,
So give it your very best shot,
Oh please, oh please give us a clue and
I'll show you what I can do!

Ashley Gregory (11)
Highfield St Matthew's CE Primary School

Everlasting Seasons

Everlasting seasons,
Give us reasons,
To thank our God,
We're all peas in a pod.

For here comes spring,
Make us all want to sing,
Baby calves born,
People mowing their lawns.

For here comes summer,
Ain't going to be a bummer,
The sun shining bright,
The Earth full of light.

Autumn is a real change,
Summer and autumn both exchange,
The bold red leaves constantly falling,
The sparrows and blackbirds making their calling.

Finally winter,
Cars beings washed with rinser,
The white floury snow drifting,
The constant breeze constantly lifting.

Adam Murphy (10)
Highfield St Matthew's CE Primary School

Night Comes

Night comes with telly speaking,
Night comes with cars passing,
Night comes with guinea pig squeaking,
Night comes with curtains closing,
Night comes with fish swimming,
Night comes to soothe me to sleep.

Bradley Price (8)
Highfield St Matthew's CE Primary School

Ellie Joe

Ellie Joe comes to stay
With eyes as gleaming as summer's day,
Ears like diamonds and teeth like snow,
A party of a girl is Ellie Joe.

Her belly is tanned, her neck is brown
And her hair is the colour of a chocolate town,
Her clothes are sure to impress
And though she is pretty she wears a pink dress.

When teacher talks she will hear everything
And shoots into work before you say a thing,
She licks the plate then asks for more
And she's even heard of a pedicure.

Ellie Joe has clean shoes,
Lives in a house and never has the blues,
She sleeps in a bed as comfy as can be
And I wish I was her and she was me.

Georgia Ascroft (8)
Highfield St Matthew's CE Primary School

Shadow

He runs when I run,
He walks when I walk,
But when I look around,
He's on the ground,
Just doing the same as me.

He moves with me,
He copies me, he follows me,
Everywhere I go,
There he is behind me on the ground.

He stops when I stop,
But every night when there's no light,
He disappears where he stands.

Johnathan Massey (10)
Highfield St Matthew's CE Primary School

Laura's In Town!

My name's Laura and I love toys,
I hate being quiet and I love noise,
I hate cats, but I love dogs,
I love sleeping, and hate doing jobs,
My name's Laura so move out the way,
I watch telly, nearly every day,
My fave biscuit has got to be a Nice,
I know they're cute on telly, but I hate mice,
My name's Laura, my name's Laura,
And before you ask, I hate butter - Flora!

Laura Rebecca Adamson (10)
Highfield St Matthew's CE Primary School

Alisha Earles

Alisha Earles comes to play
With eyes as sparkling as a summer's day,
Ears like diamonds and teeth like pearls,
A party of a girl is Alisha Earles.

Her tummy is peach, her neck is clean
And her hair is as curly as a bean,
Her clothes are enough to happily dance
And through her skirt the warm breezes prance.

Amy Duckworth (8)
Highfield St Matthew's CE Primary School

Night

Night comes with doors banging,
Night comes with dogs barking,
Night comes with clocks ticking,
Night comes with trees breezing.

Alisha Bartolini (8)
Highfield St Matthew's CE Primary School

School

S chool is cool,
C an you be a fool,
H olidays are the best,
O h you little pest,
O h come on everyone let's have some fun!
L et's see all the children playing in the sun.

Rebecca Davies (10)
Highfield St Matthew's CE Primary School

My Snake Poem

S lithering snakes everywhere,
N ever stop to have a rest,
A lways stays awake every day,
K eep an eye out for a fierce snake - be
E xtra careful in the jungle.

Joshua Cooke (9)
Highfield St Matthew's CE Primary School

School!

School is cool,
So don't be a fool,
The children are just a pest,
They play in the sun and
Have lots of fun.

Sarah Butler (10)
Highfield St Matthew's CE Primary School

The Rainbow Boy

The rainbow boy stands,
Reaching for a pot of gold,
The colours gleam bright.

Alexander Clarke (9)
Highfield St Matthew's CE Primary School

Pet Wishes

I'd love a cat
That's a matter of fact
Instead I've a bunny
And her name is Honey,
I'll keep my bunny,
Cos she's mighty funny.

I'd love a bat,
That's a matter of fact,
Instead I've a fish
And her name is Wish,
I'll keep my fish
Cos she grants my wish!

I'd love a wombat,
That's a matter of fact,
Instead I've a tiger
And her name is Fiber,
I'll keep my tiger
Cos she's made out of fibre.

Deryn Jones (10)
Highfield St Matthew's CE Primary School

The Seasons

Winter has ice,
Autumn has trees,
Spring has mice,
There's a cool summer breeze!

Winter is cold,
Autumn is wet,
Spring is bold,
Catch a butterfly in a net!

Alex Liptrot (9)
Highfield St Matthew's CE Primary School

Games

Games are fun, games are fun,
You play with them to have some fun,
Puzzle games, adventure games,
Platform games,
We play with them,
To have some fun,
Some games are good,
Some games are bad,
The bad are rubbish,
The good fantastic.

Christopher Rosbotham (10)
Highfield St Matthew's CE Primary School

Sweets

Sweets are fizzy,
They drive me dizzy,
Some are bad,
That's what drives me mad.

Chocolate is good,
Toffee is too,
It's my favourite - *Wahoo!*

Zoe Greenall (10)
Highfield St Matthew's CE Primary School

All About Me!

My name is Ash,
I think I'm cool,
I have some cash,
In the swimming pool,
My friends are weird,
Like I say,
They grow big black beards,
All through the day.

Ashleigh Wiggin (10)
Highfield St Matthew's CE Primary School

Stacey Sinclair

It's her, it's her,
It's Stacey Sinclair,
She's my best friend,
Our friendship will never end.

She's a fab friend to me,
Just wait and see,
If you see us play, we'll always say,
Play with you another day,
Whatever the day,
Whatever we play.

It's her, it's her!
It's Stacey Sinclair,
She's my best friend,
Our friendship will never end.

She's my synchronised twin,
She'll plead for her sin,
That's her, that's her,
That's Stacey Sinclair!

Lauren Lindley (9)
Highfield St Matthew's CE Primary School

Haiku

It shines like crystals,
It glows like hard steel diamonds,
It shines like glitter.

Emilie Welsby (9)
Highfield St Matthew's CE Primary School

The Sulky King - Haiku

The sulky king stands
Reaching high up in the stars,
Clothed in white bright frost.

Luke Sheridan (9)
Highfield St Matthew's CE Primary School

Night Comes With

Night comes with cars crashing,
Night comes with bikes shunts snapping,
Night comes with ants in pants,
Night comes with people talking,
Night comes with people walking.

Night comes with trees swaying,
Night comes with dogs barking,
Night comes with jewels flying,
Night comes to put us to sleep.

Jack Aspey (7)
Highfield St Matthew's CE Primary School

Night Comes

Night comes with trees blowing,
Night comes with floorboards creaking,
Night comes with clocks ticking,
Night comes with cars cruising,
Night comes with owls hooting,
Night comes with the water from the tap,
Night comes with dogs barking,
Night comes to tuck me in bed.

Samantha Critchley (8)
Highfield St Matthew's CE Primary School

Night Comes

Night comes with fish swimming in the tank,
Night comes with dogs barking,
Night comes with trains going past,
Night comes with Mum and Dad shutting the curtains,
Night comes with dads snoring,
Night comes to make you go to sleep.

Rebecca Howard (9)
Highfield St Matthew's CE Primary School

Night Comes

Night comes with dads yawning,
Night comes with owls hooting,
Night comes with dogs barking,
Night comes with clocks ticking,
Night comes with cats purring,
Night comes to tuck me into bed.

Katie Shore (9)
Highfield St Matthew's CE Primary School

Matthew Price

Matthew Price comes to the railway
With eyes as glittery as a sunny day,
Ears like swimming pools and teeth like rice,
A party of a boy is Matthew Price.

Zak Miller (8)
Highfield St Matthew's CE Primary School

Plum - Haiku

Plum you are purple,
Plum you are sweat and juicy,
Plum you're delicious.

Reece Hampson (8)
Highfield St Matthew's CE Primary School

Sunset

The golden sky gleams
Like an explosion of light
It reflects the water.

Dayna Leanne Clark (8)
Highfield St Matthew's CE Primary School

I'd Like To Be

I'd like to be a footballer,
I'd like to be a star,
I'd like to be a traveller,
Who journeys very far.

I'd like to be a skier,
I'd like to be the sun,
I'd like to be a scientist,
Who investigates upon.

I'd like to be a street racer
I'd like to be Mars,
I'd like to be a mechanic,
So I could fix fast cars.

I'd like to be a skateboarder,
I'd like to be the Earth,
I'd like to travel on a boat,
So I could jump in the sea and surf.

Whatever I'd like to be,
I'd need the help from you and me.

Christian Hardman (10)
Holy Infant & St Anthony RC Primary School

This Is Our Own Summer Place

This is our summer place
And the trees are lovely and bright,
The leaves are as green as the grass
And the river flowing swiftly
Is shining in the scorching sun.
The air is as fresh as fruit that has just been picked,
Our voices are as loud as lions' roars
And everything is as shining as diamonds.

Matthew McGrath (9)
Holy Infant & St Anthony RC Primary School

Me!

I'd like to be a little ant
And see things lower down,
I'd like to be a princess
And wear a fancy crown.

I'd like to be a cat
And jump from wall to wall,
I'd like to be a large giraffe
And see things that look small.

Whatever thing I want to be
I shan't complain because I'm me,
I'm not perfect, no one is,
The best we can do is try
And help the world, stop the wars,
Then there's no need to cry.

You should thank the Lord for all you've got,
For people who are hungry and poor,
Have no food or money
And what you have got, they have not.

Georgia Beaman (10)
Holy Infant & St Anthony RC Primary School

Heart

Happy days my little pump,
Beating when I run and jump,
Steady working day and night,
What could I do without you?
To help you what should I do?
I need you to last for years,
Though I could manage without ears,
Pump along my strongest friend
And our fun should never end.

Elizabeth Hamer (10)
Holy Infant & St Anthony RC Primary School

What Will I Be?

Will I be as funny as a clown?
Will I be a bird flying through town?
Will I be as big as a bear?
Will I be a lion with lots of fur?
Will I be able to stop war and
Find the key to the locked door?
Will I be able to swim far out to sea?
Will you be able to come with me?
Will I be able to feed the hungry,
Or maybe I should just be me?

Bethany Nuttall (10)
Holy Infant & St Anthony RC Primary School

The Highwayman

(Based on the poem 'The Highwayman' by Alfred Noyes)

The wind was like a ghostly wolf and calling to the night.
The moon was like eagles' eyes so bright, so bright.
The road was like rough seas,
To keep it steady the highwayman was using all his might.
The highwayman came riding, riding, riding,
The highwayman came riding up to the old door.

Michael Taylor (10)
Holy Infant & St Anthony RC Primary School

What I Want To Be

I want to be an angel,
I want to be a bird
And the most wonderful thing,
I want to have is freedom in the world.

Belinda Nicholson (10)
Holy Infant & St Anthony RC Primary School

When I'm Old . . .

When I'm old I want to be
A very busy buzzy bee.
I hope that there will be no war,
Only Heaven's open door.

Then I want to be a snake,
To go to sleep and never wake,
When I'd knock on Heaven's door,
Go to sleep, not even snore.

Then I'd like to be a dog,
Not even worry about a job,
I hope I have a nice owner,
That cares for me when I'm older.

Whatever God has set for me,
I hope it will make me happy.
I will work very hard at it,
I will not falter, not even a bit.

Joshua Haddock (11)
Holy Infant & St Anthony RC Primary School

My Future

I would like to be a waitress,
So I could serve you your tea,
I would like to be a sailor,
So I could travel on the sea,
I would like to be a DJ,
So I could play you a tune,
I would like to be a travel agent,
So I could book your holiday in June,
I would like to be the sun,
To send you light,
I would like to be a star,
To shine bright at night.

Naomi Sarsfield (11)
Holy Infant & St Anthony RC Primary School

Summertime

When the sun is shining
And it's the middle of June,
I think to myself,
It'll be summer soon!

Summer is a time
For having good fun
Under the beautiful
And shining sun.

So sometimes I wonder
What a marvellous thing,
Summer; the sun
And the birds that sing.

Megan Andrews (10)
Holy Infant & St Anthony RC Primary School

Hopes And Dreams

I would love to climb a mountain
With a wild breeze in the sky.
I would love to explore the Earth
And be back in record time.
I would love to help the Africans
In their time of need.

I would love to help nature
In a kind and gentle way.
I would love to swim with dolphins
And dive in and swim away.
Be happy for who you are
And what you're going to be.

Rebecca Wood (10)
Holy Infant & St Anthony RC Primary School

Will I Be A Teacher?

What will I be? Will I be a teacher?
How will I become one? I have no idea
And how will I be? Will I be nasty or nice?
Teaching is hard, it takes a lot of work.

I really want to be a teacher,
It sounds really fun.

Who will I talk to?
I won't know anyone.
Little kids running round
Laughing when they shouldn't be.

Bye teaching, because it wasn't
Exactly my thing anyway.

Sarah Shilson (11)
Holy Infant & St Anthony RC Primary School

What Should I Be?

Should I be a dog?
Should I be a cat?
Should I be a mouse?
Whatever I be I know God will love me!

Should I be a monkey?
Should I be a lion?
Should I be an elephant?
Whatever I be I know God will love me!

Should I be a dolphin?
Should I be a haddock?
Should I be a whale?
Whatever I be I know God will love me!

Eric Holliday (11)
Holy Infant & St Anthony RC Primary School

If I Was . . .

If I was a role model,
I'd have to walk up and down the aisle.

If I was a pop star,
I'd have to sing with a mike.

If I was a hairdresser,
I'd cut and style until it's right.

If I was a super girl,
I'd have to learn how to fly.

If I was a dustbin girl,
I'd have to hold my nose from smell.

If I was a vet,
I'd have to look after animals well.

If I was any of these
God would help me complete my dreams.

Briony Grant (10)
Holy Infant & St Anthony RC Primary School

I'd Like To Be A . . .

I'd like to be a fish
Who could swim in the open sea,
I'd like to be a giraffe and be
As tall as can be.
I'd like to be a tiger
Who's called Boo,
I'd like to be an otter,
Who lives in the zoo,
I'd like to be a mouse,
Who lived in a tiny house,
I cannot pick what I want to be,
Because God made me.

Laura Wright (11)
Holy Infant & St Anthony RC Primary School

If I Was . . .

If I was a super star,
I would dance and sing around the stars.

If I was a lawyer,
I would have some fun typing and writing.

If I was a dentist,
I would brush and clean those dirty teeth.

If I was a builder,
I would design and build some lovely houses.

If I was an electrician,
I would have to be efficient.

If I was a social worker,
I would bring up sick and unhealthy children.

Whatever God has set for me
I would gladly do it.

Jessica Pendlebury (10)
Holy Infant & St Anthony RC Primary School

This Is Our Summer Place

This is our summer place
And the trees are lovely
In the bright, beautiful sun.
All the leaves are crunchy green
And the river rushes down the river tops,
It is as beautiful as crystals.
The air is as fresh as fresh orange juice.
Our voices are loud and fluent
And everything is extremely peaceful.

Leonie Hazelwood (9)
Holy Infant & St Anthony RC Primary School

I Want To . . .

I want to dive with a dolphin,
Fly like a bird,
Go swinging through the jungle,
I wouldn't be scared.

I want to spy on a lion,
Catch a falling star,
Go up on to Cloud Nine
And travel really far.

I want to fly in a rocket,
Become really smart,
Own a huge grey elephant
And make a custard tart.

But wherever I go,
Whatever I be,
I will only be one person
And that is me.

Chelsie Conaghan (11)
Holy Infant & St Anthony RC Primary School

Sadness

When all turns against you,
The world leaving you out
What can you do? Oh what can you do?
All that you can do is naught.
When friendship is no more,
And all hope is lost,
Everybody is a foe,
You endure a cold frost.
You long to be happy,
But with none to be your friend,
You are not happy,
Trying to make things amend.
You cry and you cry,
Why are you sad? Oh why, oh why?

Alexandra Kelly (9)
Holy Infant & St Anthony RC Primary School

This Is Our Summer Place

This is our summer place
And the trees are lively in the scorching sun.
All the leaves are bright and green
And the river flows quickly, but quietly,
Along its river bed
And is as clear as the middle of the ocean.
The air is as clear and as fresh as snow.
Our voices are loud and clear for everyone to hear
And everything is so quiet and peaceful.

Zak Riding (8)
Holy Infant & St Anthony RC Primary School

Two Little Doves

Two doves flying high in the sky
As the days and the time passes by
Days have passed and they are still high above.
The two little birds are falling in love.
When will they ever stop flying around?
Why don't they come down to the ground?

Thomas McNair (10)
Holy Infant & St Anthony RC Primary School

Cars

Cars, cars, they're so cool
They could drive me to a swimming pool,
When I look outside to see
Cars, cars drive me to my tea.
If you don't I'll go home
And you'll never see me.

Sean Mulheran (9)
Holy Infant & St Anthony RC Primary School

Bedd Gelert

(Based on the poem Bedd Gelert)

Gelert was a very nice dog,
Liewellyn was upset.
The prince sat lonely by the bog,
He grieved about his pet.

Liewellyn was so very sad,
Thinking of times ago.
Liewellyn was so very mad,
Now his life was so low.

Hannah Castley (10)
Holy Infant & St Anthony RC Primary School

Victorian Poem

Flat caps and dresses,
Oil spills are messes.
Children in the playground,
Laughing all around.
Hopscotch and skipping,
The boys are running round nipping.
At day and night
The girls and boys are running round with their kits.

Jessica Flannery Maloney (10)
Holy Infant & St Anthony RC Primary School

School

School, school, it's so cool,
It makes learning fun,
School, school, it's so cool,
It makes education a vacation.

Luke Naylor (9)
Holy Infant & St Anthony RC Primary School

This Is Our Summer Place

This is our summer place
And all the trees are as lively as young kids
Playing in the shining sun.
All the leaves are as lovely
And as green as lovely fresh grass
And the river is clear like a beautiful crystal
And it flows really fast and you can hear
Its soothing swishing too.
The air is like fresh jungle fruit.
Our voices you can hear from miles away,
The shouting and screaming is like massive booms,
But you can hear what they are saying
And everything is under control.

Alex Forbes (9)
Holy Infant & St Anthony RC Primary School

The Highwayman

(Based on the poem 'The Highwayman' by Alfred Noyes)

The wind was a sea of rushing country air,
The moon was a glowing face without a care,
The road was a bridge over the mass of purple moor
And the highwayman came riding, riding, riding.
The highwayman came riding up to an old inn door.

The wind was a sea of ghosts, whistling through the trees,
The moon was a torch, sending out moonlight in seas,
The road was a glow stick dazzling in the core
And the highwayman came riding, riding, riding.
The highwayman came riding up to an old inn door.

Nicole Holliday (10)
Holy Infant & St Anthony RC Primary School

This Is Our Summer Place

This is our summer place
And the trees are gold as ever in the summer.
All the leaves are as green as a lime
And the river is swishing clearly,
Is as clear as crystal.
The air is as fresh as a daisy.
Our voices are as warm as the sun
And everything is as quiet as ever, today.

Jessica Ratcliffe (9)
Holy Infant & St Anthony RC Primary School

This Is Our Summer Place

This is our summer place
And the trees are colourful and very lively.
All the leaves are green as the beautiful calming grass
And the river is as clear as the light blue sky
And the children play in the bright, hot sunshine.
The air is as fresh as Africa's fresh fruit.
Our voices are clear and always want to cheer
And everything is happy and calm.
'It's summer!'

Georgie Lynam (9)
Holy Infant & St Anthony RC Primary School

This Is Our Summer Place

This is our summer place
And the trees are beautiful and green.
All the leaves are as green as grass
And the river is shiny blue and as clear as glass,
It is flowing as fast as a cheetah.
The air is as hot as the sun
Our voices are as squawking like a chicken
And everything is calm and peaceful.

Jason Nicholson (8)
Holy Infant & St Anthony RC Primary School

This Is Our Summer Place

This is our summer place
And the trees are swishing in the scorching breeze,
All the leaves are as crinkled as the sea waves
And the river is clear crystal blue,
As the waves slowly skim the side.
The air is as fresh as beautiful flowers,
Our voices are loud with excitement
And everything is perfect in summer.

Shannon Boyce (9)
Holy Infant & St Anthony RC Primary School

This Is Our Summer Place

This is our summer place
And the trees are in the happy sun
All the leaves are juicy green
And the river is swishing, why it is shining?
It is like diamonds
The air is like all different fresh fruits
Our voices are loud and clear
And everything is beautiful.

Dillon Sandiford (9)
Holy Infant & St Anthony RC Primary School

This Is Our Summer Place

This is our summer place
And the trees are as lively as children playing,
All the leaves are as green as a watermelon
And the river is as wavy as the deep, dark sea
And is sparkling clear.
The air is calm and breezy,
Our voices are loud and fluent
And everything is bright, beautiful and joyful.

Georgina Killeen (8)
Holy Infant & St Anthony RC Primary School

This Is Our Summer Place

This is our summer place
And the trees are beautiful and green.
All the leaves are as green as grass
And the river is shiny blue
And as clear as crystal.
It is as slow as snails.
The air is as hot as the sun.
Our voices are squawking like chickens
And everything is calm and peaceful.

Luke Barber (8)
Holy Infant & St Anthony RC Primary School

The Highwayman

(Based on the poem 'The Highwayman' by Alfred Noyes)

The wind was a whooshing cloud going faster than a racing car,
The moon was terrifying, staring, looking upon everything,
The road was a dusty desert
And the highwayman came galloping, galloping, galloping,
The highwayman came galloping up to the old inn door.

Bethany Taberner (9)
Holy Infant & St Anthony RC Primary School

The Highwayman

(Based on the poem 'The Highwayman' by Alfred Noyes)

The wind was like a howling wolf calling its mate,
The moon was like a gloomy world,
Ready to invade very, very late.
The road was like a winding path, dusting all around
And the highwayman came riding, riding, riding,
The highwayman came riding up to the old inn door.

Adam Liptrott (9)
Holy Infant & St Anthony RC Primary School

The Person I Want To Be

I want to be a snake that slithers all around.
I want to be a parrot that's worth a pound.
I want to be a spider that swings in the air.
I want to be a mole that runs everywhere.
I want to be a cat that jumps up walls.
I want to be a dog that always falls.
I want to be a shark, so that I can be king of the sea.
I want to be a ship, so that people can explore with me
But what I really want to be is me!

Adam Lee Reynolds (11)
Holy Infant & St Anthony RC Primary School

Animal Life For Me

I would like to be a bird,
So I could fly above the sea.
I would like to be a pig,
So I could roll up in the mud.
I would like to be a dolphin,
So I could swim all night and day
But right now I'm me
And that's the best way I can be.

Nicole Jones (11)
Holy Infant & St Anthony RC Primary School

Myself

M um and Dad love me,
Y our peace surrounds me.
S tars guide me,
E vil is away from me,
L ife leaves me.
F ish feed me.

Ryan Kelly (11)
Holy Infant & St Anthony RC Primary School

Me And My Vocation

Should I be a clown or leech?
Should I use my head and teach?
Should I be a bird and fly?
Should I sing a lullaby?
Should I be a janitor?
Should I run a kilometre?
Should I be a bumblebee?
Should I go and work at sea?

Whatever I do I'll try my best.

Elizabeth Shepherd (10)
Holy Infant & St Anthony RC Primary School

Colours Of Cars

When I travel in the car,
I watch the other cars go past.
I see different colours go by,
Like yellow, blue and green cars.
I like looking at blue cars the best,
The green cars go fast, *50 miles per hour.*
Yellow cars shine on the road,
All the other cars drive safely like my dad.
My favourite car is a blue Honda driving past me.

James Rogers (9)
Moorside Community Primary School

The Great Fire Of London

I can see houses burning in the street
Flames of light
The streets full of fire
People running away.

Benjamin Hyman (7)
Moorside Community Primary School

Elves In The Park

What can I see?
I can see a pole in the frost
A slide in the snow
A skateboard ramp in the spring
A fence in the summer.

What can I feel?
The grass shaking
The cold climbing frame
Daffodils waving from side to side
Leaves falling off the trees.

What can I hear?
Branches on the trees snapping
I can hear the daffodils singing and waving to the side
Fence rattle together - so hard
The wind blowing on the slide.

Lauren Gaskell (9)
Moorside Community Primary School

Fairy In the Castle

What I can see:
A golden chandelier hanging from the pink ceiling.
A pink wooden door with a golden doorknob.
A sparkly vase on a sparkly window ledge.
A big window with a golden light coming through.

What I can feel:
I can feel smooth, sparkly pink and gold tiles on my feet.
Soft, furry carpet tickling between my toes.
The wind blowing past my face.

What I can hear:
I can hear birds singing up in the treetops.
Wind blowing and whistling.
People talking about things.

Georgia Gaskell (9)
Moorside Community Primary School

Kennings

Coffin dweller
Garlic hater.

Cape wearer
Fang biter.

Blood eater
Cross disliker.

Pray hunter
Human killer.

Dark lover
Bat transformer.

Bone collector
Body taster.

Jack Lewis (9)
Moorside Community Primary School

Kennings Poem

Sea dweller
Fish eater

Ink squirter
Fast swimmer

Eight legger
Stinky fella

Big and yellow
Tentacle waver

Crab crusher
Water pusher.

Kieran Reason (9)
Moorside Community Primary School

Dog Kennings

Bone eater
Stick chaser

Four-legged
Cat fighter

Flea scratcher
Quick paddler.

Kennel dweller
Bark louder.

Good sniffer
Great listener.

Basket sleeper
Jaw snapper.

Tail wager.

Keyleigh Storey (9)
Moorside Community Primary School

Horse Kennings

Big kicker
Small muncher

Large footer
Lazy sleeper

Mini rider
Hay eater

Saddle wearer
Little scrapper.

Aaron Smith (9)
Moorside Community Primary School

An Elf In The North Pole

What I can see:
Sparkling white snowflakes falling.
Footsteps in the deep, dark snow.
The moon shining straight in my eyes.
Our green hats swaying in the breeze.

What I can feel:
The wind blowing on my body.
White icicles dripping on me.
The cold, breezy weather making me chilly.
The magic sprinkles tickling me.

What I can hear:
The *ho, ho, hos* loud and cheer.
Snowdrops plopping on the ground.
Children's thank yous because they got loads of gifts.
Elves talking loud about gifts.

Lauren Bullock (9)
Moorside Community Primary School

Witch In A Swamp

What I can see:
Birds calmly swooping across the sky
The beautiful sun shining high
Muddy ponds around the house
Active frogs leaping over the old couch.

What I can feel:
Horrid spiders crawling up my legs
Puddles of mud splashing on my bed
Sadness running through my brain
Splashing of the pouring rain.

What I can hear:
Frogs going ribbit in the sun
Birds singing lullabies just for fun
Seagulls flapping their wings so high
The noise of happy hunters saying goodbye.

Shannon Jenkins (8)
Moorside Community Primary School

A Fairy In A Field

What I can see:
Beautiful and colourful at the end of the field,
Dogs running with their owners,
Boys playing football and scoring goals,
Blueberry bushes having their blueberries picked.

What I can feel:
The wind swishing from side to side in the sunshine,
Leaves tickling my cheeks,
The flower petals touching me gently.

What I can hear:
The birds flapping their wings as they fly high in the sky,
The breeze of the wind going *whoosh, whoosh,*
People laughing as they play happily,
The leaves rustling on the branches.

Zoe Flannery (8)
Moorside Community Primary School

The Ogre In The Swamp

What I can see:
The swamp in front of my hut,
My green self when I look in the mirror,
All the brown trees in front of my hut,
The birds flying over the hut.

What I can feel:
I can feel my green skin,
The wind when it blows,
My hairy green chin,
The door when I walk out.

What I can hear:
The birds singing in the morning,
The fish diving in the lake,
The wind whistling through the trees,
The leaves falling off the trees.

Daniel Hallam (9)
Moorside Community Primary School

The Second World War

Tired soldiers in the war,
Some are dead on the floor.
Machine guns are shooting mad,
Against the enemy who are bad.
I can smell the smoky fire,
And the smoke fire sails up higher.
Army tanks are rumbling round,
Soldiers falling to the ground.
We won the war and I got into a plane,
And now I can resist the pain.

Kyle Doherty (10)
Moorside Community Primary School

The Great Fire Of London

I can see . . .
Huge red flames
Leaping to buildings
And ripping them down
People searching for their families
In the big, hot buildings.

Kane Magrath (7)
Moorside Community Primary School

Fear

Fear is black.
Fear tastes like sour sweets.
Fear smells like dusty rooms.
Fear looks like a haunted house.
Fear sounds like creaking doors.
Fear feels like clattering bones.

Kyle Weedall (11)
Moorside Community Primary School

Wrestlers

I can see a crowd
who are cheering very loud.
Also, I can see a referee,
who is always watching over me.
I feel very excited
and the crowd will be delighted.
I go up to frog splash Kane,
but when I get there he's hurt his brain
and he is in pain.

Corey Hardiman (9)
Moorside Community Primary School

Laziness

Laziness is light yellow,
It tastes like bacon on toast
And smells like Sunday roast dinner.
Laziness looks like breakfast in bed,
It sounds like classical music.
Laziness feels like a hot bubbly bath.

Luke Weedall (11)
Moorside Community Primary School

Fear

Fear is red,
Fear tastes like sour drop sweets,
Fear smells like rotting rubbish,
Fear looks like a scary clown,
Fear sounds like creaking floorboards,
Fear feels like falling off a cliff in a dream.

Carl Wright (10)
Moorside Community Primary School

Pop Star On Stage

When I walk on the stage
I see
The flashing of the lights
That keep following me.
And all the background dancers
Wearing shiny, sparkly clothes
Dancing so lovely that they keep in their rows.

When I walk on the stage
I feel
All lively and excited
It can't be real
I'm shaking with fear
Because it's oh so scary too
And you don't know what to do.

When I walk on the stage
I hear
All the screams and the whistles
And the shouting of the crowd
As they cheer
'Come onto the stage,' they shout
As I am walking out.

Daniella Dreha (10)
Moorside Community Primary School

Kennings Poem

Mouse chaser
Fish eater

Basket dweller
Collar wearer

Bad swimmer
Fast runner

Miaow maker
High jumper.

Fern Roberts (8)
Moorside Community Primary School

Dragon Kennings

Bone cruncher
Fire breather

Cave dweller
People frightener

Death helper
People cooker

Head remover
Body halver

Animal killer
Skull cracker

Body snatcher
Brave fighter

Angry fella
Wing weaver.

Reece Taylor (9)
Moorside Community Primary School

Kennings Poem

Cat chaser
Wall jumper

Walk lover
Food eater

Bone biter
Sock chewer

Bone hider
Toy chewer

Good digger
Noisy chewer

Stick finder
Bark maker.

Erin Wells-Lakeland (9)
Moorside Community Primary School

A Fairy At The Bottom Of A Garden

What can I see?
The green grass swishing on the floor.
The white fence blowing on the floor.
The gold door sitting there.
A white window opening and shutting.

What can I feel?
Green, soft grass blowing on the floor.
I can feel the grass on my feet.
A gold door on my house.
The rain dripping on my body.

What can I hear?
The birds making a noise.
I can hear the door opening and shutting.
I can hear the trees blowing in the wind.
I can hear the letterbox opening and shutting.

Kimberley Gaskell (9)
Moorside Community Primary School

Stella Artois

(Inspired by 'Kensuke's Kingdom' by Michael Morpurgo)

S tella Artois, oh my Stella, my dog.
T hen thy Stella washed ashore.
E ndless rage of the sea.
L ong ago she used to bark.
L oner, a loner on this island.
A lone, thy Stella was not alone.

A n old man found thy Stella.
R aging over tummy pains.
T hy Stella and me, dying for food.
O h no! Thy Stella dying for milk.
I n this world no electricity.
S tella spots a boat, I wave, it was Mum and Dad, row Dad, row!

Nina Ellen Rooney (9)
Moorside Community Primary School

Deer In A Wood

What I can see:
Hunters marching to kill an animal
Green grass full of mud
Tall trees all around
Lumberjacks cutting up tall trees.

What I can feel:
The gunshots from the hunters' shotguns
The crunch of frosty grass on my feet
The rough feel of trees on my hands.
Vibrations from the falling trees

What I can hear:
The bangs of hunters' shotguns
The lumberjacks singing a merry tune
The swishing sounds of the slim stream
Birds flapping in the sunny sky.

Stephanie Rochford (8)
Moorside Community Primary School

Orcs In A Forest

What I can see:
Little creatures crawling away from me,
Trees bending quickly side to side,
Seeing the kids playing on the old, rusty trees,
Seeing the sun brightening up the forest.

What I can feel:
The raindrops dripping all over me,
The roughness of the dark forest floor,
The wind booming in my black face,
Coldness all over my skin.

What I can hear:
The owls singing on a high brown branch,
Mice scattering across the ground,
The river flowing into the dark, dark forest,
The wind blowing trees going side to side all the time.

Connor Sanderson (8)
Moorside Community Primary School

All Alone

I can see
Furry cats, fluffy cats,
White cats, black cats
All looking at me.

No space to run around,
No trees,
Nothing to eat,
I feel scared
Here on my own.
Cats can't stop looking at me.

Can't wait to go home
With my owners.
Happy and joyful,
But for now I am lonely.
Strange faces but happy faces
Coming to feed me.

At last my owners have come for me,
Going home safe at last.

Sophie Hughes (9)
Moorside Community Primary School

A Tiger In The Jungle

I see the tiger asleep
Orange with black stripes
Trees all around
In the jungle.

I feel scared because
The tiger can wake up and attack me
And happy because
I am by my favourite animal.

I can hear all the animals and birds
Whispering *lions*.

Angela Veeres (10)
Moorside Community Primary School

Wrestling

My name is Hidenrike
And I am on my bike.
I can see Undertaker doing the chokeslam,
What is this? The wall just went *kablam*
Oh it is Kane
And he is bringing the pain.

Here is John Cena,
He is in the arena.
Here is Big Show doing the chokeslam from Hell,
The sweat off him makes a horrible smell.
And The Rock is doing the people's elbow,
Oh hey, it is Eddie Guerrero.

I can hear Ray Mysterio,
Taking on Big Show.
The crowd is chanting,
Big Show is panting.
He can't take any more
And now he is on the floor.

I can feel much pain
Coming from the punches of Kane.
Also from the leg lock
Performed by The Rock.
And someone is on their bike,
Oh! it's me, Hidenrike.

Christopher Delves (9)
Moorside Community Primary School

Fear

Fear is the colour of black like a burglar breaking in.
Fear tastes like a sour lemon.
Fear smells like green gunge if you're having a nightmare.
Fear looks like a couple of people wearing black all over.
Fear sounds like someone tiptoeing up the stairs.
Fear feels like a nightmare falling off a cliff.

Kayley Hadwin (10)
Moorside Community Primary School

Fairy In A Palace

What I can see:
Pretty pictures on the walls,
Be there when my mother calls,
In the kitchen smells lovely food,
And that makes me in a happy mood.

What I can feel:
The softness of my princess bed,
And the crown that sits on my head,
Furry rugs under my feet,
And my shiny hair which is very neat.

What I can hear:
My high heel shoes clopping on the floor,
Another loud knock on the royal door,
The miaow of my kitten,
Who plays with my mittens.

Ellie Burges (9)
Moorside Community Primary School

Happiness

Happiness is like a bright yellow.
Happiness is like a smiling sun.
Happiness makes people giggle.
Happiness feels like roses in my face.
Happiness sounds like a bubbling bath.
Happiness tastes like hot chocolate.

Mica Dale (11)
Moorside Community Primary School

Pixie In The Wood

What I can see:
Lots of trees next to my pixie house,
Loads of grass in the woods,
A road close to my house,
Animals in the woods.

What I can feel:
Thorns on the ground,
A tree stump of a tree,
Wind across my face,
The wet grass going into my shoes.

What I can hear:
The owls going *tu-whit tu-whoo* next to me,
Branches snapping when I stand on them,
The rain hitting the floor,
Pixies close to the road.

Owen Lewis (8)
Moorside Community Primary School

Anger

Anger is walking in your house and standing on a pin.
Anger is fireworks screaming all around you.
Anger tastes like chilli sauce melting in your mouth.
Anger feels like blazing fire in your head.
Anger smells like a pepper bomb up your nose.
Anger feels like you have just died.
I am *anger.*

Billy Swindells (11)
Moorside Community Primary School

Kennings Poem

Bloodsucker
Spot maker

Fast flyer
Smelly infector

Small creature
Good dodger

Blood hoover
Scab picker

Dung eater
Sand dweller

Light bulb crawler
Crumb eater.

Isaac McCarthy (8)
Moorside Community Primary School

The Haunted House

Once upon a time in the haunted house
There was a slimy, little mouse.
The mouse saw a scary man
And he got in the scary man's van
And squeezed out the gap
And landed near a spooky house
And went to the spooky man's house.
In the spooky house
The spooky man killed the mouse
And the mouse came back to life
And went back to the house
And killed the scary man and bought the house.

John White (8)
Pinfold Primary School

The Ghost Of Mrs Powder

There was a caravan site called Seaweed Bay,
It was a sort of country and western, there was a lot of hay.
There were campers from all over the land,
All the children played in a pit of sand.
The owner Mrs Powder loved the site,
Because a lot of the people flew a kite.

While she was moving the windswept lawn,
Her leg came off and it was completely torn.
Everybody was running in extreme shock,
Fifty years later there came a little knock.
She opened the door, there were two men,
She said they had to sleep in a small pen.

They went to sleep in a bit of a shock,
All night long they heard a ticking of a clock.
when they got up they found a leg,
Mrs Powder started to beg.
She took the leg and said, 'Thank you.'

'Are you scared' I'm not! Boo hoo.

Heidi Brown (10)
Pinfold Primary School

Spooky Lane

I was walking down the lane at night,
There wasn't even a street light.
There was rats running all over the place,
One of the rats even bit my face.
Scary bats were flying,
I heard kids crying.
Ahhhhh! a skeleton jumped on me,
But that was all I could really see.
I woke up in my bed,
It was just all in my head.

Portia Taylor-Black (8)
Pinfold Primary School

Phantom Of The Opera

There was once an opera house,
In the cellar, there was not a mouse.
There was someone else in the cellar,
He was a strange looking fella.

So people met up at a meeting
And said hello with a pleasant greeting.
Suddenly they heard a bang,
While everything went dark with a twang.

Oh it's only the ghost,
He stands by the post.
Even the people don't come back,
We have to give the singers the sack.

But all the people were wrong
As a man sung his song.
There was a boy who lived there all his life,
All alone without a wife.

Nicole Wilson (8)
Pinfold Primary School

The Bell

Once there was a very rich man
Who hired an architect. He was called Dan.
He came and sketched the land
And he got the builder to give him a hand.

And the man made a sign for the hotel,
It said in big letters, *The Bell*.
But nobody came to stay
Because the whole thing was the wrong way.

So he went to the stair
And looked with a glare.
He threw himself down
And hit his head on a chair.

Alisha-Dawn Kent (9)
Pinfold Primary School

The Spooky, Derelict House

There's a spooky, derelict house,
Nothing goes there not even a mouse.
I wouldn't go there,
Unless you want a scare.

I saw a googly-eyed ghost,
I saw it there as I was standing by the lamp post.
It started to charge at me,
I hid so it was me it couldn't see.

I didn't want to stay,
I wanted to go away.
My friends would call me a wimp
But at the moment I was going limp.

So there's a spooky, derelict house,
Nothing goes there not even a mouse.
I wouldn't go there,
Unless you want a scare.

Jade Ellis (10)
Pinfold Primary School

The New Extension

The extension is finished,
All the excitement of the building is amazing,
Walking downstairs the smell of paint,
The new carpet
Enters your nose.
Walking through the doors
It is like the room is wrapping its arms round you,
Everything is miniature,
Miniature red computer chairs.
The walls are full of happy, joyful pictures
Showing their delight of happiness.
The building is happiness.

Gabby Dunbar (10)
Rivington (VA) Primary School

The Deadly Art Vampire

The red blood art vampire is coming at noon,
He's bringing paint and chalk soon
And blood and flesh,
With bones and hearts dripping from its paws.
He's red, hairy and smells too,
He's quite bad, blooded tempered
And he squirts blood at you!
He eats chalk and red paint too
And paintbrushes galore.
He'll often eat paint and teachers a lot more!
He likes to muddle up people's hearts,
He makes weird noises to make them amusing
And we said, 'Oh no! He'll drink our blood.'
And the teacher said, 'I don't think he will!'
The red blooded art vampire is coming at noon,
He's bringing paint and that's soon . . .

Megan Bate (8)
Rivington (VA) Primary School

Seaside

Splash, splash,
The water splashes,
The big waves,
Surfboarding,
Swimming,
Splash
Against the rocks,
Spray on the boats,
Swish in comes the tide,
The sun goes down,
The moon comes out,
The lilos sail away
And out of sight.

Jessie Swift (10)
Rivington (VA) Primary School

The New Extension

Slowly bit by bit I walk in,
Before I do I smell the fresh paint
And the brand new carpets,
I open the red shiny door,
I hear laughing,
I feel like a giant in a room of little people
And little things.
Busy doing lots of things,
Drawing,
Painting and games,
Lots of other things too,
Little house,
Dolls' house,
Reading corner
And mini computers.
I really don't want to return,
I have to pass the red shiny door back to school,
I feel normal again, because the school is much bigger,
Just like me!

Francesca Turner (9)
Rivington (VA) Primary School

New Extension

Extension, extension,
As the blue carpet leads to the red doors,
When you walk in; the two flat-screen computers
With red computer chairs,
The children playing everywhere.
The playhouse full of fresh air,
The little couch and the displays on the wall.
The tiny world full of toys,
The little children on yellow, red and blue chairs.

Thomas Sargent (10)
Rivington (VA) Primary School

Quadbikes

The churning of the motor,
The pressure of the throttle
As I rake up the freshly laid grass
And pause for a breath.
Smelling the fumes of where I have been
As the headlights show the way.
Breaking the speed limit, quick pull the brakes,
As I halt at the end of my path,
Open the gates,
As another journey awaits
On the path I follow.

Drew Mulholland (9)
Rivington (VA) Primary School

Skiing

Skiing down the mountain,
Cold air blowing in your face,
Crisp snow, no one's been on,
Blue sky, white snow, freezing cold,
Chilly wind, whoooo down the mountain first,
Get back to a nice hot fire.

Melissa Heaton (9)
Rivington (VA) Primary School

The New Extension

I walked through the shiny red doors,
Instantly the rich smell of paint took my breath away,
I saw the clean new carpets.
On the brightly coloured walls,
There were all the months in a year.

Adina Clayton (10)
Rivington (VA) Primary School

The Extension

The school's hunched in a corner, feeling empty and alone,
Builders trickling cement into the walls,
Working away for a year and a day,
School watching helplessly at the new building,
Starting to feel even older,
Maybe even a glint of jealousy,
But suddenly he began to see,
An eruption of noise and laughter
And started to feel the buzz of curiosity.

When he peers in
He feels a giant to this land,
The extension reaching out his hand
And suddenly the school feels part of the fun,
Instead of feeling glum,
The smell of happiness and the other new things,
Makes him want to sing.
So now when you visit the school,
Instead of seeing one lovely building, shadowed by the trees
You'll see two buildings singing in the wind.

Zachary Howe (10)
Rivington (VA) Primary School

The New Extension

Walking down those echoing steps,
Happy feeling walking in,
New smell of fresh paint,
Children playing, laughing, reading,
Small computers, tiny chairs,
Mini tables, their own toilets.
Painting, drawing, cutting and sticking,
Colourful work, lots of storage,
Reading corner, painting corner, writing area,
Lots of toys, dressing up, tiny, cute new pegs,
New windows and a disabled toilet.

Jessica Myers (10)
Rivington (VA) Primary School

Early Years Unit

Children laughing in the morning.
Mrs Case teaching little children,
Older children working hard in their lessons.
School waking up, peering over
At his new friend, smelling the paint.
The foundation stage opens its eyes,
Reception learning some more words
While school has a great chat,
Fog is bouncing off the school like a battle in place,
School is protecting the extension.

Patrick Snape (10)
Rivington (VA) Primary School

Football Crazy

The players run out on the pitch
Looking both determined and ready,
Warming up for the big match,
The teams looking very sturdy,
Tension building up now,
As two players walk to the middle
The ref puts the whistle to his mouth
And *blow! blow! blow!* he whistles.

Jack McVey (10)
Rivington (VA) Primary School

The New Extension

Exploding children,
The eruption of new life,
The fiery fun.

Part of the family,
Children playing on the floor,
Cars, dolls and lots more.

Ashley Unsworth (10)
Rivington (VA) Primary School

Extension

I walk in the new extension
Feeling like I'm a giant
Or they're all dwarfs.
Everything's so tiny,
I'm just so tall.
The fresh smell of newness
Surrounds me like never before.
I walk through the new extension door,
The teacher looks so tall when she stands near them all.
New computers glisten in the daylight,
Water gets splashed out of the water play area.
I guess at one time we all must have been this small.

Rochelle Khan (10)
Rivington (VA) Primary School

Doctor Kennings

Body tester
Germ killer
Prescription writer
Advice giver
Hope dasher
Flesh cutter
Life saver.

Siân Walters (11)
Rivington (VA) Primary School

The New Extension

Dear Builders,
　　The new extension big and new,
　　Children playing, having fun,
　　Lots of lovely things to do,
　　A lovely little playground all thanks to you.

Helena Carter (9)
Rivington (VA) Primary School

The New Extension

New building is here,
It is great,
You would say so too.
Everything made for little children,
Little chairs,
Mini tables,
Mini computers,
Mini settee,
Everything is mini,
Even their own quiet reading area.
Alphabet, numbers, all around,
Reading out 1, 2, 3,
Reading out a, b, c,
Just fabulous.
Smell the new paint, smell the new floor, carpet,
New everything, playing with Play Doh, jigsaws and games.
Teacher playing with the children, reading, talking to them.
Mrs Davis looking after them,
Screaming, laughing, talking, running, skipping, painting,
Splodging, doing so much stuff all at once.
Windows sparkling, floor shining,
Their own playhouse, their own café, dressing up one by one,
Playing mums and dads.
Different colours red, blue and green,
Everything different colours.
I wish I was in playgroup or nursery
And I could be in there.

Abbi Fazackerley (10)
Rivington (VA) Primary School

The Numeracy Monster

The numeracy monster is coming today,
He's bringing times tables and equal signs to play
And fractions and shapes with sums dripping from his claws.
He's yellow and green and smelly all over,
He's very short-tempered and he burps at you.
He eats people's maths' books and pens and pencils galore.
He'll often eat rubbers, but teachers more.
He likes to muddle up sums to make them confusing.
We said, 'Oh no! he's dribbling division!'
And the teacher said, 'Quick we'll get him in prison.'
The numeracy monster is coming today,
He's bringing times tables and equal signs to play!
He's bringing . . .

Safron Newhouse (8)
Rivington (VA) Primary School

The Literacy Vampire

The literacy vampire is coming today,
He's bringing nouns and adverbs to play
With verbs and words, with books dripping from his fangs.
You'd better be careful cos he has a gang.
His teeth are so sharp, he might even . . . bite your head off!
He's got a bad temper and he smells of rotten eggs.
He loves to eat the pencil leads
And eat the children's legs.
He muddles up your homework to make it quite confusing,
He makes up weird poems to make English amusing.
We cried, 'Help he's going to give us extra homework.'
'It will do you good,' the teacher said with a smirk.
The literacy vampire is coming today . . .

Joe Roberts (9)
Rivington (VA) Primary School

The New Extension

Everybody's happy
In the new room,
To see all small things,
Feel like a giant.
The smell hits your face,
Smells rich like leather.
Everything's so small,
I have to crouch down
To wash my hands.
Corner chairs on the carpet,
Lots of new technology.
Tiny swivel seats
Because they are too small for stools.

Nicole Marsh (10)
Rivington (VA) Primary School

In The New Extension

In the new extension
The toilets are really small,
The tiles are shiny and new,
It smells like carpet and paint,
The tables are miniature, so are the chairs
In the new extension.

In the new extension
Children laugh and play,
The windows are as shiny as small stars,
Reception sit on swivelling chairs playing on flat-screen computers
In the new extension.

Hannah Bethell (10)
Rivington (VA) Primary School

The New Extension

Happy children playing and working
Like a shiny new bought shoe,
An extra piece of key added to fit the school lock,
Children sit on miniature computer chairs,
Playing with new technology,
Newly painted red doors,
Small built sinks and toilets,
Chairs and tables too.
Spongy, comfortable seats
Smelling of new leather,
Decorated bathrooms with
Shiny new tiles.

Sophie Whittle (10)
Rivington (VA) Primary School

The Ghost Monster

The ghost monster is coming today
And he eats everything in his way.
He will eat them up from top to bottom,
With tricks and games he's really rotten!
He likes to scare people and say, 'Wooo, wooo, wooo.'
It really works, they run away too!
He hangs around old, scary houses with cracked windows and
broken doors,

He hides in the ancient wardrobes.
The ghost monster is coming today
And he's eating everything in his way.

Heather Lamb (7)
Rivington (VA) Primary School

The English Vampire

The English vampire is coming today,
She's bringing horrid, scary stories for us to do!
And spellings for me and you, with letters dripping from her paws.
She's multicoloured and furry,
Believe me when I tell you it's something you would not adore.
She's quite bad tempered, as well as that she's a pain
And completely insane and thinks it's a game!
She eats the school writing books, pens and pencils,
She likes pens best, she likes the ink dripping from her mouth!
She'll often eat the teachers without a doubt.
She likes to muddle up spellings to make them confusing.
We said, 'Oh no Miss! She will eat you!'
And the teacher said, 'Quick phone the Alphabet Zoo!'
The English vampire is coming today,
She's bringing horrid, scary stories for us to do . . .

Abigail Preston (8)
Rivington (VA) Primary School

The History Ghost

The history ghost is coming today,
He's bringing myths and legends to play
And kings and queens with knights in shining armour.
He hangs around with mummies,
He's turquoise made and his nose is runny!
He's very bad-tempered and burps at you!
When he looks at you he makes your eyes pop out.
He'll often hang around with his Viking gang
Who raid the pencils, rulers and crayons at night.
'Oh no the ghost will get you,' we said.
Like Queen Elizabeth he said, 'Off with your head.'
Suddenly the ghost said, 'Boo!'
The history ghost is coming today,
He's bringing myths and legends to play . . .

James Morris (8)
Rivington (VA) Primary School

The Dinner Lady Monster

The dinner lady monster is coming today,
She's burping smelly cabbage and gloupy soup to play
And soggy chips and greeny burgers
With tomato juice dripping from her paws.
She's orange and brown and stinky too,
She's very, very bad-tempered and burps at you.
She eats the bowls, the plates, the forks and even the knives.
She makes them eat their greens, which is rather quite mean.
She likes to mix and glower around the soup to put us off our food.
She mixes different foods together and I think it's rather rude!
And we said, 'Oh no, she'll make us all eat slime.'
And the teacher said, 'Just ring dinner lady helpline!'
The dinner lady monster is coming today,
She's bringing smelly cabbage and gloupy soup to play . . .

Amber Edmundson (8)
Rivington (VA) Primary School

The History Monster

The history monster is coming today,
He's bringing Egyptians and Greeks today
And pyramids and armour,
With ancient artefacts dripping from his hands.
He's orange and slimy and smelly too,
He even gets angry when he's bad-tempered too.
And he even burps at you!
He eats history books and pencils galore,
He'll sometimes eat rulers and ruins more.
He likes to ask questions to make them confusing,
He makes toy Greek soldiers to make them amusing!
And we said, 'Oh no! He'll eat all the history books.'
And the teacher replied, 'Quick get the monster hook!'
The history monster is coming today,
He's bringing Egyptians and Greeks today . . .

Ben Possible (9)
Rivington (VA) Primary School

The Football Headed PE Teacher

The football headed PE teacher is coming today
With man-eater balls and bats to play,
And cones and mats to play with too,
He might even throw a ball at you.
He's made out of wood,
He's intelligent just like Jonny Wilkinson!
He's quite short-tempered, he loves tackling children,
He burps in class and throws hoops at children.
He eats crunchy cereal bars and drinks energy drinks
And he says, 'Oh Miss we're terrified.'
'Well phone the Rugby Zoo,' she replied.
The football headed PE teacher is coming today,
With man-eater balls and bats to play.

Matthew Seddon (8)
Rivington (VA) Primary School

The PE Monster

The PE monster is coming today,
He's bringing balls and peaches, what shall we play?
And shorts and tops with PE bags hanging from his claws.
He's big and brown and smelly too,
He's quite short-tempered and burps at you.
He eats balls and skipping ropes and mats even more,
He'll often eat children and teachers.
He likes to muddle colours of balls,
He pops little balls and big
And we all said, 'The PE monster is making us do dance!'
And the teachers said, 'Please give him a chance!'
The PE monster is coming today,
He's bringing balls and peaches, what shall we play?

Joshua Knowles (8)
Rivington (VA) Primary School

The History Mummy

The history mummy is coming today,
He's bringing ancient artefacts and sacred tombs to play.
And ancient paintings, also Greek myths
With Roman armour oozing from his bandages.
He's orange with red polkadots.
He's extremely bossy and too big for his boots!
And he likes to wrap you in bandages.
He often eats history books and ancient Egyptian posters as well
And likes to eat the teachers.
Muddles up our paintings of the Greeks,
He likes to eat the timelines and pens.
And we said, 'Oh Miss please help us!'
And she said, 'Don't worry I will phone up the dump yard.'
The history mummy is coming today,
He's bringing ancient artefacts and sacred tombs to play . . .

Tanya Bass (9)
Rivington (VA) Primary School

Off Into Space Today

Off into space today,
It's dark and enormous in the Milky Way.
There are planets and stars and aliens too,
You need to watch out or they might zap you.
The planet Zarro has the strangest creatures,
They have three heads and four eyes and other strange features.
They tried to take our ship but we said, 'No way!'
We sent them into the core of Zarro, there they will stay.
Off into space today,
It's dark and enormous in the Milky Way.

Alex Morris (9)
Rivington (VA) Primary School

The Science Bat

The science bat is coming today,
He's bringing torches, chemicals and games to play.
And liquids and solids with different oils dripping from his claws.
He's green, gooey and smelly too.
He's quite bad-tempered and he even burps at you.
He drinks and eats poisonous liquids and science books galore.
He'll often eat rulers and teachers more.
He likes to muddle words up to make them confusing,
He makes different chemicals to make them amusing.
And we said, 'Oh no, he will eat you.'
And the teacher said, 'Phone the zoo.'
The science bat is coming to today,
He's bringing torches, chemicals and games to play.

Eleanor McVey (8)
Rivington (VA) Primary School

The Art Monster

The art monster is coming today,
She's bringing colours and paints to play,
And crayons and pastels with paper from her paws.
She's blue and red and fluffy too,
She's very bad-tempered and squirts glue at you!
She eats paint brushes or one or two and chalk galore,
She'll often eat pencils and children more!
She likes to muddle paint to make them confusing,
She makes weird pastels to make them amusing.
And we said, 'Oh no! she'll eat you!'
And the teacher said, 'Don't worry, we'll phone the zoo!'
The art monster is coming today,
She's bringing colours and paints to play . . .

Eleanor Strang (8)
Rivington (VA) Primary School

The Music Monster

The music monster is coming today,
He's bringing rhyme and rhythm to play
And instruments and music notes
With tunes dripping from his paws.
He's yellow and spotty,
He's very good-tempered, has perfect timing.
He'll eat music papers and books galore
(Only music ones!)
He'll often play the piano, flute or trumpet,
He likes sorting tunes to please Miss Melody
And messing up the music files - that won't please her.
The music monster is coming today,
He's bringing rhyme and rhythm to play . . .

Emma Harrison (9)
Rivington (VA) Primary School

The Art Monster

The art monster is coming today,
He's bringing paint brushes to play
And colour and papers with beads dripping from his paws.
He's green, scruffy and smelly too,
He's quite bad-tempered and squirts glue at you!
He eats pictures, pastels and sequins galore,
He'll often eat gel pens and teachers more!
He likes to muddle crayons to make them confusing,
He makes glittering shapes that are really bemusing!
And we said, 'Oh no! He will eat you!'
And the teacher said, 'Quick put him in the art cupboard too!'
The art monster is coming today,
He's bringing paint brushes to play . . .

Bethany Hughes (8)
Rivington (VA) Primary School

The Maths Monster

The maths monster is coming today,
She's bringing shapes and numbers to play
And clocks and rulers with times tables dripping from her claws.
She's pink and purple spotted and she really smells!
And pulls tongues out at you.
She likes to eat maths books and shapes too.
She really likes teachers and children.
She counts all the time
And never gets sums wrong!
She always gets 10 out of 10 in her tests.
The maths monster is coming today,
She's bringing shapes and numbers to play . . .

Roseanna Feeney (7)
Rivington (VA) Primary School

The Naughty Monster

The naughty monster is coming today,
He's bringing silliness and a bag of worms to stay
And talking and laughing when he shouldn't be!
And wonderful jokes! Putting eyeballs in the teacher's tea!
He likes to push people in dirty puddles,
he gets your shoelaces all in a muddle.
He ate my homework but the teacher doesn't believe me!
He hides people's lunches and I get the blame.
It's never my fault, it's always the same.
The naughty monster is coming today,
He's bringing silliness and a bag of worms to stay . . .

Kelly Nightingale (8)
Rivington (VA) Primary School

The New Extension

Builders working on the playground
While Mrs Davies' teaching,
Children counting away,
The children just love the fun and work!
Tiny toilets, tiny chairs, tiny tables, tiny sinks,
We feel like we're in Lilliput Land!
You come out of the room,
Don't know where you are,
Then see the old school again.

Chloe Townsend (9)
Rivington (VA) Primary School

Cubs

My favourite thing of all is Cubs,
As long as my dad has paid my subs.

Tuesday night I rush my tea,
There's fun in store - that's a guarantee.

The best is a weekend camp,
Let's hope the tents are not damp.

To gain a badge is my aim,
Even if it means working in the rain.

The journey home takes so long,
To fill our time we sing a song.

The driver stops and parks our bus,
I look out of the window - I can see a fuss.

Oh no, it's my mum - she's having a weep,
I'm going to pretend I'm fast asleep.

Elliot Saunders (9)
St John's RC Primary School, Bolton

I See A Dog

I see a dog
At the end of the hall wagging his lively tail,
His claws scratch the floor
Louder and louder and louder,
Trying to run away from torture,
Torture is having a shower!

Drip, drip, drip, drip,
His long and curly hair
All over the place.
Races around the place,
Shoots upstairs and runs in my room.
I see a nose as black as soot
In a pile of clothes,
Delighted as ever.

Tara Vinden (9)
St John's RC Primary School, Bolton

I See A Bird

I see a bird
flying in the sky
like a butterfly,
flying swiftly.
It swoops from
branch to branch.
All day long
singing like
an angel,
his golden feathers
gleaming in the sun.

Bradley Marlor (8)
St John's RC Primary School, Bolton

White Horse

If I were a white horse
Pacing a country lane,
I would roam the place all day
In the wind and rain.

If I were a white horse
Working on a farm,
I would work day and night
And never cause alarm.

If I were a white horse
In the king's troop,
Every time I won a war
I would prance and whoop.

If I were a white horse
Running the Grand National,
I would win Grandpa's bet
Making him quite emotional.

Tejal Shanbhag (8)
St John's RC Primary School, Bolton

I See A Horse

I see a horse
Whose coat is as white as snow
And his mane and tail feel like silk
He travels as fast as lightning
As he gallops along the track
He is kind and friendly
He listens when you say something
Whining and snorting.

Charlotte Howarth (8)
St John's RC Primary School, Bolton

I See A Dog

I see a dog,
Panting at the park
With a very loud bark.
Off he goes! Fetching a stick. *Run! Run!*

He jumps as high as a giraffe,
With a coat as green as grass.
His nose sniffing in the ground,
Off he goes! Giving back the stick. *Run! Run!*

Time to go home
Out the gate,
Down the road,
Through the door. Off he goes! *Run! Run!*

With fur like silk,
The colour of milk.
Eyes drooping,
Bedtime now, up he goes! *Run! Run! Sshh!*

Oliver Burns (8)
St John's RC Primary School, Bolton

I Have A Fish

I have a fish
Swishing around in its tank,
Its scales look black as night,
Glimmering in the light,
But at night it hides in its cave.
Swimming all day,
Up and down its tank
And rests at night.

Liam Ryan (8)
St John's RC Primary School, Bolton

My Puppy

I love my puppy, he's silly and fluffy,
We play together all day long,
Throwing and catching his ball, he's full of energy,
Running and racing and I'm the one doing the chasing.

I love my puppy, he's brown with white spots,
Just like a Dalmatian, but not!
He has a long bushy tail and eyes so cute,
But we still tell him off when he chews Dad's boots.

I love my puppy, he's like my best friend,
Always pleased to see me, playing till the day ends,
We've been together all our lives,
Like the sun and the moon high up in the skies.

Phillipa Tinker (8)
St John's RC Primary School, Bolton

There's The Cat

There's the cat chasing the mouse
Sneakily running, chasing the mouse
With wide eyes which are black
They shine like buttons in the sky
Smashing the ornaments while chasing the mouse
Suddenly he strikes.

Matthew Clarkson (8)
St John's RC Primary School, Bolton

I See A Horse

I see a horse, his coat is as black as coal.
I see a horse, his tail sways like a tree in the breeze.
I see a horse, his eyes sparkle like the stars.
I see a horse, his mane is as soft as silk.

Victoria Rozdziabyk (9)
St John's RC Primary School, Bolton

I See A Fish

I see a fish with shining orange scales,
I see a fish swimming around going nowhere,
I see a fish making a popping noise,
I see a fish going on a broken ship,
I see a fish called Fred.

I see a fish yellow like the sun,
I see a fish swimming in the rocks,
I see a fish with four fins,
I see a fish playing in the shells,
I see a fish called Velmao.

Emma Hunt (8)
St John's RC Primary School, Bolton

Winter Brings . . .

Winter brings snow . . .
Winter brings ice . . .
Winter brings fun . . .

Winter brings cries of joy and happiness,
Winter brings the glorious birthday of Jesus Christ our Lord,
Winter brings a happy and glorious spring close behind.

Nicole Rodgers (9)
St John's RC Primary School, Bolton

I See A Cat

I see a cat curled in a ball
He's always on the look out
Like a soldier with binoculars
He's always after mice
Like a motorbike
But when he sees a dog
He's as fast as a rat.

Jacob Cooper (8)
St John's RC Primary School, Bolton

I See A Horse

I see a horse
Prancing ready to go
With his black coat, smooth as gold.
His hooves like metal shining in the sun.
He canters through the gate.
He waits patiently swaying at the starting line.
He nods his head to get ready
Ready, steady, go!
Off and away he gallops.

Rebecca Povall (8)
St John's RC Primary School, Bolton

I See A Dog

I see a dog
slowly panting in the bright green grass
just before the big race.
Her hair as short as toothbrush bristles
glistening in the sun.

While she was waiting she barked and whimpered.
Her brown eyes gleaming in the bright sun,
then suddenly they're off!

Sean McQuaid (8)
St John's RC Primary School, Bolton

I See A Fish

I see a fish swimming joyfully
Whizzing around the tank looking for me
Gold skin shining in the water
Blowing bubbles on his way
    I see a fish looking for me.

Ellie Edginton (8)
St John's RC Primary School, Bolton

I See My Rabbit

I see my rabbit jumping around very happily
Running up and down the stairs with glee
And she is white and she is brown
And she is very, very friendly
I like the rabbit I see
Because she cuddles up to me
Watching TV
I see my rabbit.

Jack Cullen (8)
St John's RC Primary School, Bolton

I See My Cat

I see my cat
chasing a bird
creeping up slowly
ready to pounce
his fur is really furry
his colour's black and white
he's hissing like a snake
trying to catch the bird.

Thomas Pilling (8)
St John's RC Primary School, Bolton

I See A . . .

I see a dog, a dog that is as black as night,
It's as good as gold,
It is soft and furry,
It has floppy ears, paws and a tail,
It also growls and yelps,
Its tail swishes like a horse,
It can fetch a ball and a stick.

Peter McGowan (9)
St John's RC Primary School, Bolton

I See A Hamster

Cuddling up in a little ball
Crushing his seat down below
He looks like a polar bear
And has a pink and white nose
He eats nuts and runs on his wheel
And crawls around my bed and cuddles up with me
He doesn't stay for tea
But lives at home with me.

Brittany Bennett (8)
St John's RC Primary School, Bolton

I See A . . .

His fur is as black as coal
He is as soft as snow
His eyes are as shiny as stars
His nose is wet
His pink tongue licks my hand
He is called Dexter
He is my rabbit.

Tom Greenhalgh (8)
St John's RC Primary School, Bolton

Rabbits!

I have a rabbit, it's soft, black and white.
I have a rabbit, it sometimes gives me a fright.
He may bump his head,
He has long and floppy ears,
We've had him for two years.
His name is Sutty,
Sometimes I think he's nutty!

Emily Unsworth (8)
St John's RC Primary School, Bolton

I See . . .

I see my dog Baxter
Sitting at the bottom of the stairs
Looking at his lead
Getting all excited
Waiting for his walk
Whimpering and weeping
His bright eyes sparkling.

Now we are ready
He is running to the door
His tail wiggling more and more
On with his collar
Click with his lead
Onto the field
Running with the breeze.

Emilee Fullaway (9)
St John's RC Primary School, Bolton

I See . . .

I see . . .
Rover the dog,
He leaps and jumps,
He runs and bumps
All over the place.

He's as brown as a tree
And as black as coal.
He walks like a cat
And runs like a tiger.

His fur is short,
He's made for sport
And oh how fast he is!

Daniel Hill (8)
St John's RC Primary School, Bolton

Crazy Animals

There once was a crock called Snapper,
Who ate a mouldy cracker,
He let out a scream and his teeth turned green,
And he fell in the pool with a splatter.

There once was a monkey called Dunc,
Who burped until he stunk,
He wore one shoe and his nose was blue,
And he lived in a big tree trunk.

There once was a squirrel called Reg,
Who liked his meat and two veg,
While rooting for nuts he fell up to his guts,
In a very prickly hedge.

There once was a rhino called Clive,
Who liked to jump off the high dive,
One day he fell off into a pig trough,
And was never again seen alive.

Sam Rooney (10)
St Mark's CE Primary School, Ormskirk

My Baby Sister

My baby sister called Izzy
Is always so busy
She laughs all day
And says,
'Please may I have a twizzy?'

My baby sister called Izzy
Likes getting dizzy
She runs all day
And I have to get out of her way
As she shouts, *'Wizzy, wizzy, wizzy!'*

Emily Gibbs (9)
St Mark's CE Primary School, Ormskirk

Hurricane

I can't be halted, I languish when I feel.
I'll murder, I crush anything I admire.
So what if I make destruction with my senseless fingertips?
People, vans, houses,
I don't caution.
As my stomach whirls like the inside of a blender.
Bodies crushed like bananas.
My uniform is resplendent,
For I'm a soldier for Mother Nature.

Calum Williams (10)
St Mark's CE Primary School, Ormskirk

My Family . . .

Right, let's start,
There's Daddy who is always in a paddy.
Then there's Mummy who is really *very* funny.
There's my little sister Hatty who's really rather scatty.
Then it's my little, little sister Immy who is very silly.
There's Grandad with all his little handbags,
And my grandma who likes to drive the car.
Oh, and then there's me who's, well, perfect!

Olivia McCoombe (9)
St Mark's CE Primary School, Ormskirk

Love

L ove is about sweetness
O nly you and me
V alentine's presents
E ven you and me.

Ashley Oldfield (9)
St Mary's Catholic Primary School, Scarisbrick

Fun, Fun, Fun

School is meant to be fun,
Teachers say it all the time,
Stop complaining this is meant to be fun,
Here's a fun maths test to do,
'Let's all watch a fun educational video,' they say,
But to be truthful, it's not fun at all,
That's why they invented playtime,
But then they invented the wall!

Alexander Blundell (10)
St Mary's Catholic Primary School, Scarisbrick

Fun, Fun, Fun

Happy, joyful, playful fun
Laughing, playful, dizzy fun
Challenging, happy, funny fun
Joyful, joking, laughing fun
Dizzy, funny, silly fun.
Fun, fun, fun!

Steven Ashton (11)
St Mary's Catholic Primary School, Scarisbrick

Fun, Fun, Fun

Fun sounds like children laughing,
It tastes like a brownie going into your mouth,
Fun smells like a flower,
It looks like a doughnut,
Fun feels like a can full of fun.

Fun, fun, fun!

Liam Hesketh (11)
St Mary's Catholic Primary School, Scarisbrick

Darkness

Darkness is black and dull,
A room that is dark sounds like a creak from a floorboard,
Rooms that are dark taste dry but slimy,
Dark rooms smell like a pile of muck,
A dark room looks like an attic,
Darkness feels like a ghost,
The dark reminds me of a professional host.

I hate darkness,
It creeps me out,
Sometimes it makes me scared,
But I just hate the darkness.
Darkness is horrible,
I hate it.

Max Hindle (10)
St Mary's Catholic Primary School, Scarisbrick

Darkness

Darkness is black and gloomy like a witch,
It tastes like horrible, stale food running down my stomach.
Darkness sounds like the floor of the landing cracking,
Also with the smell of dead spiders lying on my bedroom floor.
It looks like a witch trying to hurt me,
The feeling is like a big slap on my face.
The scary darkness reminds me of the rock band.

Georgia Berry (9)
St Mary's Catholic Primary School, Scarisbrick

Fun

Fun is for cool swimming in a swimming pool,
having a lovely tropical orange drink,
taste the ice, it makes your mind go nice,
then laugh at your friends having head lice,
    that's what you all fun.

Robert Hilton (10)
St Mary's Catholic Primary School, Scarisbrick

Love

Love, where would we be without love?
No one could love anything,
People would hit and hurt each other,
Instead of hug and kiss,
People would live alone,
And some would live on the streets,
Valentine's Day wouldn't exist,
Animals would scratch and hiss,
But worst of all fun would not be fun.

Alex Alderdice (10)
St Mary's Catholic Primary School, Scarisbrick

Fears

My fears are all mixed up,
I don't know what to think,
My head is all muddled up,
And I still don't know what to think.

My fears are in my body,
And they are all around me,
I wish I was so brave,
Then all my fears would be gone.

Nicole Cronin (10)
St Mary's Catholic Primary School, Scarisbrick

Hate

Hate is red like a bursting volcano,
It sounds like fire hissing.
Hate tastes like red-hot chilli peppers,
And it smells like smoke,
And looks like burning fire.
It feels like jagged rocks.
Hate reminds me of death.

Elliot Ryder (10)
St Mary's Catholic Primary School, Scarisbrick

The Fun . . .

The *fun* of driving is you can go very fast,
The *fun* of playing with your mates is the games,
The *fun* of school is when it has been and passed,
The *fun* of being a celebrity is all the fame.

The *fun* of football is scoring a goal,
The *fun* of dancing is the Saturday night fever,
The *fun* of writing is . . .
Nothing at all!

Wallace Louise Berry (11)
St Mary's Catholic Primary School, Scarisbrick

Fun

Fun
So good and interesting
It is not as boring as reading
Fun is playing a game
Or having a joke with a friend
But not shopping for fashion
Or even the latest trend.

Frank Sharratt (9)
St Mary's Catholic Primary School, Scarisbrick

The Funfair

The roller coasters are fast
and the candyfloss is nice
and you will see a man there juggling fifty mice.
The games are really fun
and the sweets are very good
but the best thing at the funfair
is you can get covered in mud.

Adam Jordan (9)
St Mary's Catholic Primary School, Scarisbrick

Hunger

H elp people who stare
U nderstand how they live
N ow please offer them food
G ive them something to drink
E normous amount of people die
R ead this and just *help!*

George Sargent (10)
St Mary's Catholic Primary School, Scarisbrick

Tsunami Poem

T hailand, India, Africa, Sri Lanka,
S ome were demolished to pieces.
U nder the water there was an earthquake,
N ow everything, objects, houses are gone,
A nimals, insects, plants, birds all washed away,
M any lives were ruined or even lost,
 I hope this will never occur again.

Ejiro Kevu (11)
St Mary's CE Primary School, Hawkshaw, Bury

My Poem

T sunami is terrible,
S ave them,
U nforgotten,
N o friends, no family,
A big scene,
M ust help them,
 I t's terrible.

Josh Dudley (8)
St Mary's CE Primary School, Hawkshaw, Bury

School's Menu Of The Week

Jade's juicy jam,
Sadie's silly sausages,
Rebecca's red radish,
Hannah's horsey ham,
Courtney's crunchy crisps,
Shannon's stupid strawberries,
Ben's biting bananas,
Jordan's jumping jelly,
Tom's tossy tomatoes,
Liam's lazy lemons,
Mrs Woodward's walking Wotsits,
Anthony's angry apples,
Melissa's moody melon,
Natalie's nutty nuts,
Courtney's crunchy cakes.

Stephanie Belk (9)
St Mary's CE Primary School, Hawkshaw, Bury

Pet's Picnic

Rat's rotten raspberries,
Rabbit's red radish,
Dog's dodgy dumplings,
Cat's crumbly crunchies,
Pony's peppermint Polos,
Guinea pig's greasy gravy,
Fish's flat flan,
Bird's brunchy bread,
Sheep's soggy salad,
Pig's prepared peas,
Cow's cotton candy,
Hen's honey ham,
Lion's lovely lime,
Tiger's tempting teacakes,
Giraffe's giddy gum.

Jordan Tipping (9)
St Mary's CE Primary School, Hawkshaw, Bury

Family Food

Courteney's crunchy carrot,
Hugo's hairy hamburger,
Leah's lovely lolly,
Ryan's rotten rice,
Mum's mighty melon,
Dad's dairy dumpling,
Paul's precious peas,
Nana's naughty noodles,
Grandad's gorgeous grapes.

Courteney Kiely (8)
St Mary's CE Primary School, Hawkshaw, Bury

My Sense Poem

Silence is white like a newborn lamb in spring,
It tastes like a cold glass of milk,
It looks like the sun in spring.

It feels like sheep wool,
It sounds like a lamb after it's born,
It smells like freshly cut grass,
It reminds me of spring on my farm.

Joseph Phillips (10)
St Mary's CE Primary School, Hawkshaw, Bury

My Sense Poem

Fun is yellow like playing in the sun,
It tastes like fruit pastilles,
It looks like a brand new football,
It feels like getting a hat trick,
It sounds like a cheer,
It smells like glory,
It reminds me of Man United winning.

Tom Robinson (10)
St Mary's CE Primary School, Hawkshaw, Bury

My Sense Poem

Darkness is black like a shadow of a spider,
It tastes like snakes' venom,
It looks like a broken light in the room,
It feels like spiders' hair,
It sounds like a scream,
It smells like the cold,
It reminds me of going to bed last night.

Guy Loxham (9)
St Mary's CE Primary School, Hawkshaw, Bury

My Sense Poem

Darkness is grey like a shark in the moonlight,
It tastes like gravel in mud,
It looks like eternal slumber,
It feels like a sore punch,
It sounds like the creeping of skeletons,
It smells like a rusty nail,
It reminds me of fear!

Hamish Fraser Fleming (7)
St Mary's CE Primary School, Hawkshaw, Bury

My Sense Poem

Anger is red like a Nazi flag,
It tastes like rotten ketchup,
It looks like blood on my finger,
It feels like a door being slammed in my face,
It sounds like shouting and arguing,
It smells like a pool of blood,
It reminds me of hitting someone.

Adam Purves (10)
St Mary's CE Primary School, Hawkshaw, Bury

I'm Scared

I'm scared of Coke and I'm scared of Pam,
I'm scared of sticky jam,
I'm scared of bats and I'm scared of cats,
I'm scared of feathery hats,
I'm scared of cats and I'm scared of dogs,
I'm scared of long bats,
I'm scared of friends and I'm scared of pens,
I'm scared of big, fat hens.
I'm getting better though,
I'm not scared of Kate anymore!

Nicole Rigby (8)
St Mary's CE Primary School, Hawkshaw, Bury

My Sense Poem

Anger is red like boiling blood,
It tastes like burnt sausages,
It looks like a house with no windows,
It feels like a volcano getting hotter and hotter,
It sounds like the world is going to explode,
It smells like a rotten egg,
It reminds me of my mum shouting at me.

Shannon Wilkinson (9)
St Mary's CE Primary School, Hawkshaw, Bury

My Sense Poem

Darkness is as black as a rubbish bag,
It tastes like dirt,
It looks like a cannonball,
It feels like me falling into a black hole,
It sounds like a pencil sharpening,
It smells like blood,
It reminds me of a spooky graveyard.

Courtney Freeman (10)
St Mary's CE Primary School, Hawkshaw, Bury

My Sense Poem

Love is a delicate shade of pink,
like a heart-warming smile.

It tastes like chocolates,
posh and sweet.

It looks like love hearts,
pink and neat.

It feels like a soft, warm kiss.
It sounds like a frost-covered chiming bell,

It smells like roses,
red as lipstick.
It reminds me of a wedding ring,
a symbol of love.

Lisanne Mallinder (10)
St Mary's CE Primary School, Hawkshaw, Bury

Friends' Food

Steph's soggy sausages,
Sadie's silly salad,
Jade's jumping jelly,
Jordan's joggy jelly beans,
Hannah's horrible ham,
Anthony's angry apricots,
Liam's levitating lime,
Jack's jolly jellyfish,
Mum's melting melon,
Conor's crunchy cakes,
Rebecca's red radish,
Adam ate apples
Courtney's crispy corn flakes,
Mrs Woodward's walking Wotsits.

Rebecca Pearson (9)
St Mary's CE Primary School, Hawkshaw, Bury

Tsunami

T sunami is a huge wave, thousands died,
S ome managed to survive, but not many,
U nsuspecting families lost their lives,
N obody yet knows how many have gone,
A nimals could sense it but people couldn't,
M any managed to get away but they were hurt,
I hope they can rebuild their lives.

Hollie Ashworth (11)
St Mary's CE Primary School, Hawkshaw, Bury

Tsunami

T ragedy, terrible news and tidal waves,
S uffering people because of no clean water,
U nhappy people with no food, people lonely, and orphans
   wandering around,
N o homes for people to live in,
A ngry people are upset because of the dead,
M any were killed,
I hope the tsunami will never happen again.

Ese Kevu (8)
St Mary's CE Primary School, Hawkshaw, Bury

Tsunami

T is for tsunami,
S is for saved people,
U nbelievable loss and despair,
N o food, no homes, no family,
A great disaster,
M is for mending lives,
I hope it never happens again.

Conor O'Neill (9)
St Mary's CE Primary School, Hawkshaw, Bury

I'm Scared Of . . .

I'm scared of toads and I'm scared of frogs,
I'm scared of mice, rats and dogs,
I'm scared of cows and I'm scared of pigs,
I'm scared of skeletons and sparkly wigs,
I'm scared of hair and I'm scared of butter,
I'm scared of falling down in the gutter,
I'm scared of clowns and I'm scared of wasps,
I[m scared of a rabbit that hop, hop, hops.
I'm getting better though,
I'm not scared of myself anymore!

Emily Baker (11)
St Mary's CE Primary School, Hawkshaw, Bury

My Sense Poem

Fear is grey like a rat in the sewers,
It tastes like bitter fish,
It looks like a skeleton hanging from its neck,
It feels like a bowl of spiders,
It sounds like someone screaming forever,
It smells like smoke from a cigarette,
It reminds me of a seriously scary nightmare.

Victoria Hui (10)
St Mary's CE Primary School, Hawkshaw, Bury

Freaky Food

Monsters' mouldy munchies,
Ghosts' gross golden syrup,
Frankenstein's fat Frosties,
Vampires' vile Vimto,
Dracula's dirty duck,
Loch Ness monster's lumpy lollies.

Harry Edward Dixon (8)
St Mary's CE Primary School, Hawkshaw, Bury

I'm Scared Of . . .

I'm scared of fish and I'm scared of frogs,
I'm scared of desks, mags and logs,
I'm scared of bats and I'm scared of books,
I'm scared of eyes, lips and cooks,
I'm scared of rulers and I'm scared of water,
I'm scared of my auntie's daughter,
I'm scared of teeth and I'm scared of pens,
I'm scared of chickens and even hens,

I'm getting better though,
I'm not scared of windows anymore.

Bethany Smith (10)
St Mary's CE Primary School, Hawkshaw, Bury

My Sense Poem

Fear is red like a devil with red horns,
It tastes like blood-red blood,
It looks like horns, red horns,
It feels like a tap on both shoulders,
It sounds like feet, loud feet,
It smells like smoke,
It reminds me of a dark room and very loud feet.

Georgina Gloster (7)
St Mary's CE Primary School, Hawkshaw, Bury

My Sense Poem

Fun is pink like a party dress,
It tastes like melting chocolate,
It looks like different colours of balls,
It feels like when I go in a bubble bath,
It sounds like people playing,
It smells like a cook cooking,
It reminds me of my family.

Madeline Allanson (8)
St Mary's CE Primary School, Hawkshaw, Bury

I'm Scared

I'm scared of bats and I'm scared of cats,
I'm scared of all animals, but really rats,
I'm scared of Mum and I'm scared of Dad,
I'm scared of Dad when he gets mad.
I'm scared of ghosts and I'm scared of the dark,
I'm scared of even going to the park,
I'm scared of rain and I'm scared of Mum when I get done.

I'm getting better though,
I'm not scared of paper anymore!

Molly Phillips (8)
St Mary's CE Primary School, Hawkshaw, Bury

I'm Scared

I'm scared of cats and I'm scared of dogs,
I'm scared of bats and even logs,
I'm scared of people and I'm scared of toys,
I'm scared of books and frogs and boys,
I'm scared of balls and flies,
I'm scared of the dark and eyes,
I'm scared of my mum and I'm scared of tape,
I'm scared of Dad and even grapes.
I'm getting better though,
I'm not scared of boxes anymore.

Kate Smith (7)
St Mary's CE Primary School, Hawkshaw, Bury

My Sense Poem

Fear is fed like blood,
It tastes like a bug,
It looks like a monster,
It feels like a slug,
It sounds like fire,
To remind me of darkness.

Lars Christopherson (7)
St Mary's CE Primary School, Hawkshaw, Bury

I'm Scared

I'm scared of apples and I'm scared of pears,
I'm scared of even going down the stairs,
I'm scared of Mum, I'm scared of Dad,
I'm scared of Dad when he's really, really mad.
I'm scared of fish, I'm scared of cats,
I'm scared of dogs and really black bats.
I'm scared of school, I'm scared of home,
I'm scared of my brother having a big moan.
I'm getting better though,
I'm not scared of the TV anymore!

Jessica Bailey (9)
St Mary's CE Primary School, Hawkshaw, Bury

I'm Scared

I'm scared of my friends and I'm scared of my pens,
I'm scared of feathery, clucking hens,
I'm scared of ducks and I'm scared of books,
I'm scared of my sister's ugly looks,
I'm scared of Mum and I'm scared of Dad,
I'm scared of my mum getting so mad,
I'm scared of girls and I'm scared of boys,
I'm scared of old smelly toys,
I'm getting better though, I'm not scared of paper anymore!

Bethany Kay (8)
St Mary's CE Primary School, Hawkshaw, Bury

My Sense Poem

Love is red and pink like roses,
It looks like someone kissing,
It feels like goosebumps going up someone's spine,
It sounds like classical music,
It smells like lavender bubble bath,
It reminds me of a girl and a boy sitting on a bench.

Sadie Grecian (10)
St Mary's CE Primary School, Hawkshaw, Bury

Class Crunchies

Rebecca's red radish,
Sadie's silly sausages,
Liam's lousy lemons,
Jack's jumping jelly beans,
Courtney's crunchy crisps,
Stephanie's soggy salad,
Antony's angry apples,
Jordan's jogging jelly,
Conor's camping cakes,
Hannah's honey ham,
Adam's annoying anchovies.

Jade Johnston (10)
St Mary's CE Primary School, Hawkshaw, Bury

Football Food

Beckham's bacon burger,
Ljumberg's lovely lolly,
Rooney's red radish,
Scholes' sugary sweets,
Ronaldo's ripe raspberries,
Howard's horrid ham,
Van Nistelrooy's vital vinegar,
Carrol's creamy custard,
Butt's beautiful butter,
Neville's nice nuggets.

Alex Walker (8)
St Mary's CE Primary School, Hawkshaw, Bury

Tsunami

T ragic tidal wave,
S cenes of despair,
U nder the sea,
N o homes, no friends and no families,
A mazing escapes,
M ending bones,
I hope it never happens again.

Eleanor Hamer (8)
St Mary's CE Primary School, Hawkshaw, Bury

Blue Watch

B is for Blue Watch.
L is for liquid like H_2O.
U is for using fire engines.
E is for emergency.

W is for water.
A is for appliance.
T is for teaching young children.
C is for clothes that they wear.
H is for hoax calls at 20%.

Iqra Asghar (10)
St Peter's CE Primary School, Bury

Friends

F riends forever
R emember what they're for
I f they're upset help them
E veryone be friends
N ever fall out
D readful times, stick together
S o stay friends.

Liam Wood (10)
St Peter's CE Primary School, Bury

Football Crazy

Football crazy, football mad,
Except when I lose, I feel really sad.
We never lose, we always win,
Except when the balls get kicked in the bin.
We like winning, we like fun,
We only like winning when we're in the sun.
We always roll
When we get a goal.

Darcey Pearson (10)
St Peter's CE Primary School, Bury

Animals

Dogs, dogs, I love dogs,
They're always friendly like humans.
I wish I could have one,
Dogs, dogs, dogs.

Cats, cats, I like cats,
They play with their own toys.
They don't like vets,
Cats, cats, cats.

Jodie Thornley (9)
St Peter's CE Primary School, Bury

Tarantulas

They're creepy and scary,
Their legs are so hairy.

They bolt and they scurry,
They clash and they hurry.

They bite and they pinch,
If they bite you you'll flinch.

David Rimmer (9)
St Peter's CE Primary School, Bury

The Dreaded Dinner Ladies

They emerge from the kitchen round about nine
You start the school day thinking you're fine
It gets to eleven and you really want food
You see what's on offer, now you're not in the mood,
The pasta is cold, the ice cream is not
It's not really much to want your pasta to be hot.
They slop on the cabbage, watery and green
Come out dinner ladies you know you've been seen
Come out with your hands held high
Dinner ladies your end is nigh
Now that everyone's lunch is packed
Of course, the dinner ladies got sacked.

Dani Marshall (11)
St Peter's CE Primary School, Bury

Friends

Friends are always there for you,
Right by your side,
If you ever need them, they will always be there,
Everywhere you go you'll find them.
Never forget your friends, you will regret it.
Don't leave them behind,
See, friends are the best.

Leah Shepley (10)
St Peter's CE Primary School, Bury

Ocean

Ocean, ocean, all around me,
the ocean wind blows my hair across my face.
Ocean, ocean, all around us,
the sunlight shines down on us.
The ocean goes still.

Rachael Walsh (9)
St Peter's CE Primary School, Bury

Blue Watch

B lue Watch are the best,
L ots of fun to do.
U nderground floods
E very day going to fires.

W atching out for us,
A ppliances you have,
T eaching young children,
C hildren so young,
H oax calls all around us.

Lauren Dixon (10)
St Peter's CE Primary School, Bury

Friends!

F riends are the nicest things in your life,
R eally they are,
I 've known lots of friends,
E verywhere you go, they're always there,
N ever let you down,
D on't ever leave you,
S urely they are number one.

Sarah Littler (10)
St Peter's CE Primary School, Bury

My Owl

B oo Boo is an owl,
O wl that I held,
O ther owls around her.

B ut I chose Boo Boo
O f all the other owls.
O wls are my favourite animals in the whole wide world.

Thomas Ridgley (9)
St Peter's CE Primary School, Bury

Rage Against The Machine

R is for rage because they rage in their songs all night long,
A is for awesome music that they play,
G is for great guitarist, best ever known,
E is for everlasting punk.

A is for always rocking non-stop,
G is for great music played,
A is for always rocking in their hearts,
I is for incredible stuff they play,
N is for never stopping,
S is for super fast guitaring
T is for too cool for anyone else.

T is for they're always cool,
H is for having the best guitarist,
E is for every song is good.

M is for maniac guitarist,
A is for awesome singing,
C is for cool bass,
H is for higher than other bands,
I is for incredible stuff the guitarist plays,
N is for never stop their music,
E is for excellent band name.

Aston Roger (9)
St Peter's CE Primary School, Bury

My Pet

M y pet is a cat,
Y es, she likes cat food and tuna.

P urring all day,
E ating all the tuna,
T earing the settees and my bed.

James Wrethman (10)
St Peter's CE Primary School, Bury

The Playground

The playground is quiet, quiet for a time,
But at playtime it is busy, busy, like a town,
Football frenzy is on the pitch,
Girls skipping for a long time,
People fighting, it must hurt,
Ring goes the bell, everyone groans,
People rush to get into a line,
Teachers come out with a frown
Because they didn't get a new lounge,
In their staffroom of course,
So, as we go in,
I see little children waving their hands,
Ohhh! I forgot, when we get in,
Everyone has to do a *maths test!*

Ryan Heslop (10)
St Peter's CE Primary School, Bury

School

School is boring, it's for wimps,
School is boring, it's for chimps.
School can be boring, but normally it's fun!
And every lunchtime we get a chocolate bun.
There are crisps and there's chocolate and rice pudding too,
But most of the stuff looks like goo.

When I go into the classroom, our teacher isn't there,
We've got a supply teacher, her name is Mrs Wear,
Now we are doing maths and everyone is sitting down,
Most of the class have a frown.
Now the day has ended and I can go home,
My friend's phone has just gone off, I never really realised she
had such a cool tone!

Louise Cunliffe (11)
St Peter's CE Primary School, Bury

My Bedroom

My bedroom, my bedroom, what can I say?
My bedroom is a mess every day.
I once had a makeover, that went OK,
a week later it wasn't my day.
So I scrubbed, polished and even washed,
but I couldn't find the washing up liquid, even that was lost.

As my mum came home early from work,
she ran up to my bedroom, but, *oh no,*
as she walked up to my wardrobe doors, everything changed,
so I had to do it all over again.

As I finally got my room tidy with a little help from my mum,
thank God I tidied it all up soon, but something is going to go wrong,
you know what? I'm leaving soon,
my room is going to be a mess once again,
I hope my room stays tidy for ever, but I know that won't happen,
so, as I move onto my new house, everything is new, new as can be.

As my dream has finally come true, *oops,*
I think I spoke too soon.
With toys and games scattered all around me,
we can't see anything, not even my terrible room.

Jenna Vaughan (10)
St Peter's CE Primary School, Bury

Chinese New Year

The Chinese dragon is going down to town
Different colours, red, yellow and brown
Firecrackers banging
Firecrackers clanging
Listen to the music all around you
Listen! Let's join in with the dance too
Come on! Get a plate of rice
Let's add a little spice.
Kung Hei Fat Choy!

Afsheen Jamil (9)
St Peter's CE Primary School, Bury

Tass

T ass is my fat, lazy, black cat.
A hundred times he has tried and failed to . . .
S leep on my bed,
S illy cat, funny cat, my best friend.
E ating is his favourite thing to do.
L azy cat, sleeping all day.

H am is his favourite food.
O ver a bridge he runs very fast.
T assel Hot Barefoot is his real name.

B ut he is very fat.
A scratch could really hurt you.
R unning, oh, he can do that!
E at, eat, eat, that is all he can do,
F at, lazy cat.
O h he is so naughty,
O f course he goes out at night,
T una is his favourite food as well.

Sarah Green (9)
St Peter's CE Primary School, Bury

Dragon Ball Z

D ragons came from the sky
R oaring sounds from the sky
A nd all the sky goes as black as I
G ore and violence filled the land
O n the very same day he died
N ever seen before

B eing myself is as cool as immortality
A t last I was reborn as deadly as before
L ying, cheating and more
L ying on the ground there will be someone I know

Z fighters will die once more.

Jack Harris (10)
St Peter's CE Primary School, Bury

Rage Against The Machine

R is for rapid crowd
A is for awesome
G is for great drums
E is for excellent bass

A is for active lights
G is for Gibson SG
A is for action in the crowd
I is for incredible sound
N is for night-time performance
S is for straight edge
T is for tricking sounds

T is for technical stuff
H is for high stage
E is for everyone jumping

M is for mad singer
A is for awesome concert
C is for creating lyrics
H is for hosting crowds of people
I is for interesting sounds
N is for a national performance
E is for excellent show.

Conor Duthie (9)
St Peter's CE Primary School, Bury

Rabbits

R abbits are my favourite animal,
A nd I have got 6 rabbits, I love them,
B eautiful bunnies, they are wonderful,
B ut they are soft and furry.
I snuggle up to them,
T he best thing about them is they're mine.

Sophie Whittaker (9)
St Peter's CE Primary School, Bury

Dinner Ladies

D ancing, drama, dinner ladies,

I love dinner, cheese, chicken and chips.

N eed any help? Just ask Miss.

N ice is our dinner lady, she is ever so shady.

E njoyment and games, fun in the sun,

R adical races, all little faces.

L augh, join in, now might as well have some fun
whilst you're in the sun,

A person is crying, what do you do?

D inner ladies, creepy, scary, where do they go? We still don't know.

I mportant people, dinner ladies are, and deserve 3 good stars,

E verybody loves dinner ladies helping, caring and always sharing,

S uper-duper dinner ladies playing rounders although I would
rather have a ¼ pounder.

Sophie Mansell (10)
St Peter's CE Primary School, Bury

Queen

Q ueen are the first British band,

U nlike other rock bands,

E ven when the singer died.

E very other band tries to be better,

N ever die, they're Queen.

Jack Haigh (9)
St Peter's CE Primary School, Bury

Cats

C ats are cute, they make you laugh,

A t the vet's they scamper and claw.

T una is a cat's favourite food,

S o don't give them what they don't want!

Joshua Whittaker (10)
St Peter's CE Primary School, Bury

Dinner Ladies

Dinner ladies, dinner ladies,
Oh my days
One little raindrop,
'Come on kids, get inside, it's raining.'
'It was one little drop, Miss.'

Dinner ladies, dinner ladies,
What can I say?
Only one thing to say,
Can't live with them,
Can't live without them.

Dinner ladies, dinner ladies,
What the heck?
I'm surprised she's not broken her neck.
With those platform boots on
And a tiny skirt.

Dinner ladies, dinner ladies,
I can't believe my eyes,
What's on for dinner? What a surprise,
Chicken and chips followed by chocolate pies!

Gabrielle Wilson (10)
St Peter's CE Primary School, Bury

Man City

M y favourite football team is Man City,
A nd my favourite football star is Shaun Wright Phillips,
N ever cheats like Man Utd.

C ity of Manchester, best football pitch.
I t's never like when City lose, we are not bothered.
T he team I hate is Man Utd,
Y ou have to cheer when City score a goal.

Emma Hanley (10)
St Peter's CE Primary School, Bury

Playtime

Ding, dong, the clock strikes half-past ten,
We have done 2 lessons, now it's playtime again.
My friends come over to me, 'Great, let's go out to play,
I'm going out with my friends and I'm feeling OK.

Let's go and play footy, that's the best game
Except for when we lose, that is very lame.
We all pick teams and make them fair,
But we lose once again so I wish I wasn't there.

I decide to leave, I would rather play hide-and-seek,
I tell my friends to go and hide and I won't peek.
I find Dani first, she is easy to find,
We can't find Gaby but oh, never mind.
We leave her there night and day
Until next time we are ready to play.

We get fed up with hide-and-seek so we go to play tig,
When we are chasing each other, off comes Miss Lanky's wig.
We stop playing to admire the sight,
Miss Lanky with no hair on, what a fright!

We run inside and slam the door,
Thank goodness we are not playing anymore.

Dayna Crabtree (10)
St Peter's CE Primary School, Bury

Pets

P ets are warm and cuddly when they go to sleep
E ight cuddly cats in a basket
T en dogs barking in the back garden
S ix hamsters speaking in the house.

Lauren McDonald (9)
St Peter's CE Primary School, Bury

Football Mad

Man U - 2   City - 0
Man U and City are playing a match
At Man Us football ground
And kick-off's about to start
As Gary Neville starts off with the ball
And kicks it to Wayne Rooney
He takes a shot and it went in
And the crowd jumps with joy.

David James from City
Who plays in goal, jumped up to save it
It went over his head and into the net
And that's why it was 1-0.

It's half time and it's already 1-0
To the best team in the world.

The players are now ready to play this match
As Ruud Van Nistelrooy has got the ball
And kicks it to Wayne Rooney as David James
Gets the ball and kicks it in our net
And that gives us one more goal.
It's the end of the game and we've won
2-0 and the crowd jump with joy
saying,
   'Glory, glory, Man United,
   Glory, glory, Man United
   Glory, glory, Man United
   When the Reds come marching
   On, on, on!'

Becky Torr (10)
St Peter's CE Primary School, Bury

School

I wake up in the morning fresh for a new day
To work hard and play hard throughout the day
I walk in school with a frown
Because this school gets me down.

I go in the classroom to see my friends
But in comes my teacher so the conversation ends
'Sit down, sit down we're doing maths today
So hurry up, be quiet or you'll miss your play.'

'Art next, this will brighten you up,
I want you to draw a sketch of a cup.'
Nobody does, they draw the teacher,
With some very special features.

Here comes dinnertime, *yum, yum, yum*
I get to fill up my big tum.
I'll get crisps and chocolate with an apple too
What would you get if it was up to you?

Dinnertime's passed and now it's RE
But I'd much rather have PE
Everybody yawning, they hate RE
Two boys are screaming they want PE.

Home-time at last
School time has passed
I'm walking home with my friends
So my conversation will not end.

Hayley Turner (10)
St Peter's CE Primary School, Bury

Little Faith

Little faith
That's me,
Little faith,
I agree,
Little faith,
I rock,
Little faith,
I'm like a hard block,
Little faith,
I'll get on with you,
Little faith,
If you're not blue,
Little faith,
I'll make you greater,
Little faith,
See you later.

Lauren Howard (10)
St Peter's CE Primary School, Bury

Morning

Morning begins with me just walking
Morning begins with me just talking
Morning begins with the bell ringing
Morning begins with all the children lining up
Morning begins with us hanging our coats up
Morning begins with us answering the register
Morning begins with us going to assembly
Morning begins with us going back to class like crazy cats
Morning begins with Miss Gess explaining
Morning begins with getting to work
Morning ends with the tuck bell banging.

Chanice Patel (9)
St Simon & St Jude's CE Primary School, Bolton

Morning

Morning begins with the bell ringing
Morning begins with children rushing
Morning begins with everyone lining up patiently
Morning begins with answering the register
Morning begins with lining up for assembly, noisily like an elephant
Morning begins with children banging down the steps
Morning begins with waiting for assembly to begin in the great hall
Morning begins with everyone leading back from assembly
Morning begins with Miss Gess telling the class what to do
Morning begins and we're working
Morning begins with eating our tuck
Morning ends with playtime.

Ashleigh Barghuti (8)
St Simon & St Jude's CE Primary School, Bolton

Morning

Morning begins with the sun rising
Morning begins with the birds singing
Morning begins with the wind blowing
Morning begins with the bumblebees sitting on flowers
Morning begins with the trees blowing
Morning begins with children lining up
Morning begins with the register being said
Morning begins with assembly
Morning begins with a lesson
Morning begins with the tuck list being said
Morning ends with playtime.

Mehran Mokri (9)
St Simon & St Jude's CE Primary School, Bolton

Morning

Morning begins with bells ringing, *bring, bring*
Morning begins with the register scribble
Morning begins going into assembly
Morning begins with going back to class
Morning begins with starting our work
Morning begins being silent with our work
Morning begins with stopping our work
Morning begins having our tuck
Morning begins putting our coats on
Morning begins lining up outside the cloakroom
Morning begins with the bell going
Morning begins with going outside playing with our friends
Morning ends with going back to class.

Nadia Harman (8)
St Simon & St Jude's CE Primary School, Bolton

Morning

Morning begins with the bell ringing
Morning begins with the children linking
Morning begins with people pushing
Morning begins with starting the register
Morning begins with going to a peaceful assembly
Morning begins with singing a hymn
Morning begins with saying a prayer
Morning begins with getting awarded
Morning begins with children getting ready for a lesson
Morning begins with everyone listening
Morning ends and now it is the afternoon
Morning begins tomorrow like the sun goes up and down
Morning is just a peaceful bit of the day.

Daniella Seddon (8)
St Simon & St Jude's CE Primary School, Bolton

Morning

Morning begins with . . . children singing
Morning begins with . . . the bell ringing
Morning begins with . . . doing the register
Morning begins with . . . going to assembly
Morning begins with . . . coming back
Morning begins with . . . bobbles that snap
Morning begins with . . . children counting
Morning ends with teachers shouting.

Amber Barlow (8)
St Simon & St Jude's CE Primary School, Bolton

Morning Begins With . . .

Morning begins with . . . bell ringing
Morning begins with . . . children singing
Morning begins with . . . lining up
Morning begins with . . . the register
Morning begins with . . . assembly
Morning begins with . . . coming back from the hall
Morning begins with . . . teacher telling us what to do
Morning ends with . . . children eating tuck.

Hafsa Iqbal (8)
St Simon & St Jude's CE Primary School, Bolton

Morning

Morning begins with the bell ringing, *ding-dong*
Morning begins with the register doing its job and children chattering
Morning begins with the children playing like a kangaroo jumping
                                                                    up and down
Morning ends with eating our tuck.

Kishan Patel (7)
St Simon & St Jude's CE Primary School, Bolton

Morning

Morning begins with me just walking
Morning begins with me and my brother just talking
Morning begins with the bell ringing
Morning begins with the register being answered
Morning begins with going into assembly
Morning begins with me just thinking
Morning begins with tuck given out
Morning ends with a good play.

Irram Amjad (8)
St Simon & St Jude's CE Primary School, Bolton

Thunder

One day I had a wonder
Why, oh why, is there thunder?
Why does it crash?
Why does it bash?
Why does it go through the skies
To almighty highs?
Why does it have a yellow light?
Why has it got lots of might?
And I still wonder
Why is there thunder?

Roisin Wherry (9)
Whittle-Le-Woods CE Primary School

Little Robin Sitting In A Snowy Tree

When it's snowy all you can see is white
The little balls of ice sprinkle on me like pink and white confetti
I pull on my waggly wellies and set off in the snow
And guess what I see;
A little robin redbreast sitting in a snowy tree
Waggling his little bony tail, happy as can be.

Sarah Hanrahan (10)
Whittle-Le-Woods CE Primary School

Cats And Dogs!

Cats always tease dogs,
No wonder they end up hurt.
Dogs like playing games,
Especially playing in the dirt.

Cats and dogs never get along,
But if they did, I wonder what it would be like?
If cats and dogs could be best friends,
Maybe they'd share a bike.

Cats like sleeping
And dogs like eating.
They equally love to be pampered
And never left alone.

Jessica Murphy (10)
Whittle-Le-Woods CE Primary School

Football

Dribbling down the pitch
A player tackled me
In my leg I felt a painful twitch
I looked all around me
And all I could see
Was the referee shouting,
'Free kick!'

The whistle blew
I took a step back
And kicked the ball
The ball flew
What a goal!

Charlene Broomhead (10)
Whittle-Le-Woods CE Primary School

The Evacuee

The evacuee is saying goodbye
The poor little thing starting to cry.
The evacuee is on a train
The poor little thing scared of the cane.

The evacuee is saying hello
The poor little thing carrying a pillow.
The evacuee is being caned
The poor little thing struck with pain.

The evacuee is on a chair
The poor little thing eating a pear.
The evacuee has gone to bed
The poor little thing with a very sore head.

Isabelle Kennedy (10)
Whittle-Le-Woods CE Primary School

Seasons

Spring is a time when flowers grow,
Spring is a time when buds grow,
Spring is getting towards summer.

Summer is a time when you go on holiday,
Summer is a time when you sunbathe,
Summer is getting towards autumn.

Autumn is a time when leaves fall off trees,
Autumn is a time when it gets cold,
Autumn is getting towards winter.

Winter is a time when we celebrate Christmas,
Winter is a time when it snows,
Happy New Year!

Hannah Vickerman (9)
Whittle-Le-Woods CE Primary School

Brownies

At Brownies we play games
And learn each other's names.
We sing songs about God
And say yes whilst we nod.

Then we have discos and food
Which keeps up our good mood
Then happiness spreads to all.

We have water fights,
On Wednesday nights
Then we have cola and hot dogs
And then we learn about guide dogs.

Brownies should be happy, cheerful and light,
Brownies also never fight.

Josie Hull (8)
Whittle-Le-Woods CE Primary School

Months Of The Year

January's child is red and spotty,
February's child won't use a potty,
March's child is very kind,
April's child can't make up its mind,
May's child likes flowers,
June's child thinks it has powers,
July's child runs at a good pace,
August's child is full of grace,
September's child has not done a sin,
October's child was born to win,
November's child has nice hair,
December's child is a nightmare.

Emma Davies (9)
Whittle-Le-Woods CE Primary School

Cricket

Cricket is a great sport
And loads of people should play it,
Cricketers are good at the sport,
Still they keep very fit.

Michael Vaughan, Andrew Flintoff all play it
Oh what a six lad
Sometimes they're brilliant and they also score runs
But sometimes they're really mad.

The crowd turn up in rain or sun
But sometimes there is no game,
They stay a long time just in case
Then in the end they see the players of fame.

Sam Mundy (10)
Whittle-Le-Woods CE Primary School

Scary Night

As you see him in the night
He will give you such a fright
He told me his name, the king of night
Then he flew off on his kite.

When the dark becomes light
He disappears
When the light becomes dark
He reappears.

When you see his dark black cloak
You'll know it's him, he'll give you a poke.

His silver eyes shine out like a star
His hands are soft like a smooth soap bar.

Charlotte Kenyon (10)
Whittle-Le-Woods CE Primary School

Ten Little Children

(Based on 'Ten Little Schoolboys' by A A Milne)

Ten little children,
Were drinking wine,
One fell over
And then there were nine.

Nine little children,
Eating meat on a plate,
One ate it all up
And then there were eight.

Eight little children,
Went to the park with Megan,
One got lost in the woods
And then there were seven.

Seven little children,
One is called Pips,
Pips fell in the playground and hurt his knee
And then there were six.

Six little children,
Doing the jive,
One tripped over Jenny
And then there were five.

Five little children,
One bumped into the door
And fell on the floor
And then there were four.

Four little children,
One flicked a pea,
It hit Peter in the eye
And then there were three.

Three little children,
One went to the loo
Got locked in
And then there were two.

Two little children,
One flew
Into a bush
And then there was one.

One little child,
Eating a scone,
It was poisoned
And then there were none.

Heidi Clement (7)
Whittle-Le-Woods CE Primary School

Oh No!

What's happened over here?
I don't know dear
There's mess everywhere!
I'm doing my hair!

Nail varnish on the floor
And someone's knocking on the door!

What shall I wear?
I'm messing up my hair.
My boots are turning brown
And my skirt is falling down.

Make-up on the floor
And someone's knocking on the door!

Nothing left to do,
Except wait round for you,
Dad's calling round,
But I'm already down.

Nothing on the floor
And no one's knocking on the door.

Samantha Edwards (10)
Whittle-Le-Woods CE Primary School

Ten Smelly Children

(Based on 'Ten Little Schoolboys' by A A Milne)

Ten smelly children,
Standing in line,
One drinking lots of wine
And then there were nine.

Nine smelly children,
Standing at the gate,
One met a mate
And then there were eight.

Eight smelly children,
Falling down from Heaven,
One fell on Megan
And then there were seven.

Seven smelly children,
Having a good pick,
One found a stick
And then there were six.

Six smelly children,
Found a hive,
One got stung
And then there were five.

Five smelly children,
Crawling on the floor,
One fell through the trapdoor
And then there were four.

Four smelly children,
Sitting in a tree,
One fell off
And then there were three.

Three smelly children,
One turned blue
And lost his shoe
And then there were two.

Two smelly children,
Eating scones,
One broke a bone
And then there was one.

One smelly child
Soon was gone,
To the dairy
And then there were none.

Eleanor Gibson (8)
Whittle-Le-Woods CE Primary School

The Thing

Miles up in space
On the shimmering moon
There is something there
That eats kids on a spoon.

He has three huge eyes
And a big purple nose
Six long arms
And twenty wiggly toes.

He likes kids with salt
And pepper too
But if he has too much
He'll need to use the loo.

So when you're older
And you go into space
I just wanted to warn you
Just in case.

Joshua Mansfield (11)
Whittle-Le-Woods CE Primary School

Ten Silly Bunnies

(Inspired by 'Ten Little Schoolboys' by A A Milne)

Ten silly bunnies,
Standing in a line,
One got knocked off
And then there were nine.

Nine silly bunnies,
Looking at the dates,
One got hit
And then there were eight.

Eight silly bunnies,
Travelling to Devon,
One went to Heaven
And then there were seven.

Seven silly bunnies,
Eating a Twix
One swallowed a bit of the biscuit
And then there were six.

Six silly bunnies,
In a hive,
One got stuck
And then there were five.

Five silly bunnies,
Knocking at the door,
One knocked herself
And then there were four.

Four silly bunnies,
Eating their tea,
One tripped up to get to the table
And then there were three.

Three silly bunnies
Making the noise moo,
One lost his voice
And then there were two.

Two silly bunnies
Eating a scone
One practically ate a swan
And then there was one.

Lucy Gaskell (7)
Whittle-Le-Woods CE Primary School

My Horse

My horse likes eating hay,
It likes the day,
It jumps over big jumps,
It trumps when it jumps.

My horse likes going in the fields
And it likes its meals
It likes going to shows
It likes my toes
And I love my horse so much.

Dayna Bateman (8)
Whittle-Le-Woods CE Primary School

Friends Poem

I like to go out shopping with my friends
And sometimes we go to watch funny movies
We go for clothes and shoes.

We also go out for tea
It's my favourite hobby
Me and my friends play games
And do fun stuff
Shopping is the one for me.

Katie Smith (10)
Whittle-Le-Woods CE Primary School

Ten Little Children

(Based on 'Ten Little Schoolboys' by A A Milne)

Ten little children,
Drinking lots of wine
One drank too much
And then there were nine.

Nine little children,
Playing with their mates
One got bumped
And then there were eight.

Eight little children
Flying in Heaven
One fell down
Then there were seven.

Seven little children
Walking along
One saw a Twix
Then there were six.

Six little children
Doing the jive
One fell over
Then there were five.

Five little children
Walking through the door
One got lost
And then there were four.

Four little children
Walking alone
One climbed a tree
Then there were three.

Three little children
Running along
One flew away
And then there were two.

Two little children
Playing in the field
One ran away
So then there was one.

One little child
Playing on his own
He ran away
Then there were none.

Rhiannon Bennett (7)
Whittle-Le-Woods CE Primary School

Teeth

My teeth are shiny and white
They shine with all their might
They look very light
They don't like to fight
They don't dress up as a knight
They go to sleep at night
I think they are light
What a sight
They cannot fly a kite
But they can bite!

Emma Galloway (8)
Whittle-Le-Woods CE Primary School

Boxing

Boxing is really fun
Once I won
When I went to the gym
I met a boxer called Tim
I've drawn a picture of him
But he looks slim
Tim goes to the gym with his top
Tim pops the boxing bags with his hands.

Jack Gowan (9)
Whittle-Le-Woods CE Primary School

Ten Silly Children

(Based on 'Ten Little Schoolboys' by A A Milne)

Ten silly children
Standing in a line
Along came a monster
And then there were nine.

Nine silly children
Eating off a plate
They all had a food fight
And then there were eight.

Eight silly children
Running to Devon
One disappeared
And then there were seven.

Seven silly children
Mixing up pips
One ate a rotten one
And then there were six.

Six silly children
Standing alive
Along came a rattlesnake
And then there were five.

Five silly children
Shutting all the doors
Along came the nasty cat
And then there were four.

Four silly children
Climbing up a tree
One fell off
And then there were three.

Three silly children
Sitting on the loo
One flushed the toilet
And then there were two.

Two silly children
Eating a scone
One had a big one
And then there was one.

One silly child
Met his hero
After that
Then there were zero.

Samuel Mansfield (8)
Whittle-Le-Woods CE Primary School

Darkness

He came fast and sharp,
His face came out like a star.
He wandered in his nightmare,
Fearsome in a group.

His coat was your nightmare,
His hands poked your dreams.
His fingers whack your friends away,
You're left on your own,
He'll take you now.

Aashay Vaidya (11)
Whittle-Le-Woods CE Primary School

Volcano

A volcano is erupting
With a fearsome grumble and rumble
Its screaming a hissing sound
Lava is falling, hitting the ground
Fire is burning all around

Like a beast, he's so angry now
What shall we do?
'Run, shout!'

Chelsie Humber (11)
Whittle-Le-Woods CE Primary School

Ten Little Dogs

(Based on 'Ten Little Schoolboys' by A A Milne)

Ten little dogs
Sitting soft and fine
Along came a dragon
And then there were nine.

Nine little dogs
One jumped over a gate
The other dogs were still sitting there
And then there were eight.

Eight little dogs
Floating up to Heaven
One got lost
And then there were seven.

Seven little dogs
One of them had some pips
The others didn't
And then there were six.

Six little dogs
They were all alive
One did a dive
And then there were five.

Five little dogs
One saw a person and patted it with his claw
The dog ran off
And then there were four.

Four little dogs
One ran up a tree
It didn't come back
And then there were three.

Three little dogs
One stood on someone's shoe
The dog didn't care
And then there were two.

Two little dogs
One had a scone
But it had too much
And then there was one.

One little dog
Had left and gone
He never came back
And then there were none.

Rachel Hanrahan (8)
Whittle-Le-Woods CE Primary School

My Friends

My friend Jessica
My friend Jessica is nice to be with
Sometimes it sounds like she's in a myth
She likes to play football
And she scored a goal
Jessica's a very nice friend.

My friend Liberty
My friend Liberty has a very nice house
The thing is she's never seen a mouse
Her family is very nice
She's never had headlice
Liberty is a very nice friend.

My friend Ruth
My friend Ruth has a dog called Milly
Sometimes you get mixed up with Molly
Her hair is brown
She never lets you down
Ruth is a very good friend.

Laura Hannett (8)
Whittle-Le-Woods CE Primary School

What Happened To Ten Children

(Based on 'Ten Little Schoolboys' by A A Milne)

Ten little children
Hanging from a line
One fell off
And then there were nine.

Nine little children
Playing at the gate
Along came a tiger
And then there were eight.

Eight little children
On their way to Devon
On their way back one went to Heaven
And then there were seven.

Seven little children
Eating a Twix
Their mum said, 'Do you want to make a mix?'
And then there were six.

Six little children
All alive
One went away and did the jive
And then there were five.

Five little children
Lying on the floor
One says, 'Let's see your toy claw'
And then there were four.

Four little children
Saw a bee
One touched the bee with his knee
And then there were three.

Three little children
Getting some new shoes
One went to look at some other shoes
And then there were two.

Two little children
Eating a scone
Along came their mother
And then there was one.

One little child
Sitting by a pond
He fell in
And then there were none.

Nicole Richardson (7)
Whittle-Le-Woods CE Primary School

Changes

My hair is blonde
My hair is brown
My hair is black
My hair is back.

My nails are pink
My nails are gold
My nails are silver
My nails are long.

My skirt is long
My skirt is short
My skirt is pink
My skirt is black.

My boots are high
My boots are low
My boots are on
So come on, let's go.

I'm in the car on my way
Bye-bye house for another day.

Emma Pearson (11)
Whittle-Le-Woods CE Primary School

Ten Little Children

(Based on 'Ten Little Schoolboys' by A A Milne)

Ten little children
Standing in a line
The first one drank some wine
And then there were nine.

Nine little children
Saw a boy
And went on a date
And then there were eight.

Eight little children
Having a sweet at eleven
And one choked on one
And then there were seven.

Seven little children
Having a Twix
One went to the park and didn't come back
And then there were six.

Six little children
Went onto a hill
And committed suicide
And then there were five.

Five little children
Saw a hive, one went in
And he didn't come back
And then there were four.

Four little children
Were playing football
One got hurt
And then there were three.

Three little children
Were climbing up a tree
One fell back
And then there were two.

Two little children
Were skipping
One child fell over the rope
And then there was one.

One little child
Playing in the park
She had a scone
A swan ate the scone
And then there were none.

Kate McMullan (7)
Whittle-Le-Woods CE Primary School

Football, Football

I love football
It's the best
Better than all the rest.

My friends like it
Everyone goes
People sitting in the rows.

Screaming, shouting
The crowd go mad
Oi, referee, that tackle is bad.

My team are winning
It was a super goal
Davis took it round Joe Cole.

The whistle goes
Bolton win
Blackburn should be in the bin.

Liam Pearse (9)
Whittle-Le-Woods CE Primary School

Ten Big Monsters

(Based on 'Ten Little Schoolboys' by A A Milne)

Ten big monsters
Standing in grime
One got chopped up
And then there were nine.

Nine big monsters
Standing on slate
Along came a witch
And then there were eight.

Eight big monsters
Standing in Devon
One got shot
And then there were seven.

Seven big monsters
Standing on Twixes
Along came a giant Twix
And then there were six.

Six big monsters
Standing in hives
And one danced the jive
And then there were five.

Five big monsters
Standing on the floor
One fell over
And then there were four.

Four big monsters
Sitting in a tree
One fell off
And then there were three.

Three big monsters
Sitting on the loo
One fell in
And then there were two.

Two big monsters
Standing on scones
One slipped
And then there was one.

One big monster
Sitting on a scone
He ate a video
And then there were none.

Owen Grimes (7)
Whittle-Le-Woods CE Primary School

Flowers

Flowers in spring
Flowers in summer
Flowers in autumn
But never in winter.

Flowers are red
Flowers are blue
Flowers are yellow
And pink, whooooo!

There are daisies
Tulips, buttercups too
My favourite flowers
Are especially for you.

Emily Flewitt (10)
Whittle-Le-Woods CE Primary School

Little Robin Redbreast

Little Robin Redbreast
Sitting in a silver tree
Shining in the moonlight
Pretty as can be.

Lily Dickinson (9)
Whittle-Le-Woods CE Primary School

Ten Little Children

(Based on 'Ten Little Schoolboys' by A A Milne)

Ten little children
Drinking wine
One fell over
And then there were nine.

Nine little children
One met a mate
And then there were eight.

Eight little children
Flying up to Heaven
One fell down
And then there were seven.

Seven little children
Eating lots of pips
Along came a crocodile
And then there were six.

Six little children
Saw a hive
A bee stung one
And then there were five.

Five little children
Lying on the floor
One slipped over a box
And then there were four.

Four little children
Playing next to a tree
A bee stung one
And then there were three.

Three little children
One shouted boo
One was scared and ran away
And then there were two.

Two little children
Out came Tom
He took one of the children to football
And then there was one.

One little child
Saw a super hero
One stayed to spy
And then there were zero.

Quine Skillen (7)
Whittle-Le-Woods CE Primary School

Friends

We have friends
Friends who play with me
I like having friends
They're always there for me
We all have . . . *friends.*

Friends are helpful
Friends are caring
Friends are friends
And that is the end!

Chelsie Heyworth (9)
Whittle-Le-Woods CE Primary School

Friends

Friends make me jolly
And my name is Holly!
We never have a bad day
We go together like *best friends!*

Holly Magill (9)
Whittle-Le-Woods CE Primary School

Ten Little Dogs

(Based on 'Ten Little Schoolboys' by A A Milne)

Ten little dogs
Swimming in some wine
One drank all of it
And then there were nine.

Nine little dogs
Sitting on a gate
One fell off
And then there were eight.

Eight little dogs
Playing in Devon
One went to Heaven
And then there were seven.

Seven little dogs
Playing with some sticks
One got in a mix
And then there were six.

Six little dogs
Dancing to the jive
One had a drive
And then there were five.

Five little dogs
Sitting on the floor
One fell through
And then there were four.

Four little dogs
Stuck in a tree
One broke its leg
And then there were three.

Three little dogs
Sitting in a shoe
One got stuck
And then there were two.

Two little dogs
Swimming with a swan
One got lost
And then there was one.

One little dog
Chasing a frog
Then it got shot
And then there were none.

Jack Strong (8)
Whittle-Le-Woods CE Primary School

Superdog

Superdog's flying through the air,
Will he save the millionaire?
He is super, he is brave and he lives in a cave,
He has saved one million lives and twelve pies
Superdog flies through the air
He has saved the millionaire.

Superdog's work is done
So now he is sitting in the sun
But the next day he will fly away
To save the day.

Martin Parry (9)
Whittle-Le-Woods CE Primary School

My Mum Poem

M um cares about me
U ncle Bob too
M y dad loves me a bit like *you*.

Keira Skillen (9)
Whittle-Le-Woods CE Primary School

Ten Little Children

(Based on 'Ten Little Schoolboys' by A A Milne)

Ten little children
Jumping on a line
One fell off
And then there were nine.

Nine little children
Looking for a mate
Meeting at the gate
And then there were eight.

Eight little children
On a trip to Devon
Can't wait to see Megan
And then there were seven.

Seven little children
Would like to have a Twix
Mum said no
And then there were six.

Six little children
Doing the jive
One hurt a leg
And then there were five.

Five little children
Shooting to score
One broke its leg
And then there were four.

Four little children
Sailing out to sea
One fell out
And then there were three.

Three little children
One flew
Into a tree
And then there were two.

Two little children
Eating a scone
One got poisoned
And then there was one.

One little child
Trapped a finger
In the door
And then there were none.

Robson Broomhead (7)
Whittle-Le-Woods CE Primary School

The Battle Of The Nazgul

Archers feeling terrified
For they have the main part
In this, the battle of the Nazgul
It will be history.

As the Nazgul screams, it is horrific
Archers armed, warriors determined
Then it appears,
The Nazgul.

Fellowship members are in charge
So they attack first with might
And the rest of the army with fear
Close their eyes and attack.

The battle had been won
No one died
Except for the dreaded Nazgul.

James Booth (10)
Whittle-Le-Woods CE Primary School

My Pet Rabbit

My rabbit eats hay in May,
It gives him the happiest day.
And he loves to ride in the car,
He likes to listen to my guitar
And he likes to play in the hay.

My rabbit licks his paw
And he likes doing it more and more.
Sometimes he runs away
Then he goes on the grass and lays
And he messed about on the lawn today.

Megan Downs (8)
Whittle-Le-Woods CE Primary School

Football

Football is a brilliant sport,
That everyone can play.
Whether you're good or bad
Or even if you just can't play.

Before your game begins
You just do your stretches
So you're ready to play your best.
But when you play, be careful
Because injuries can occur
But join in with your friends
And you'll have the best time in the world.

Evie Sanderson (10)
Whittle-Le-Woods CE Primary School

Rice Is Nice

Beyond the sky
Way up high
On the indigo moon
There came a *boom!*
Then out came an alien dressed in green
It said, 'Hi, I'm Fancine.'
She had sixteen orange toes
And her finger was up her nose
'This is nice
So here's your rice
And here's your bill to pay
So I'll be on my way.'

Kathryn Unsworth (11)
Whittle-Le-Woods CE Primary School

My Aunt Fanny

My aunt Fanny
Lives in a vanny.
She has a grandson called Danny
Who lives with a lamby.

One day my aunt Fanny said,
'Hello Danny, have you seen my vanny?'
'No, aunt Fanny,' replied Danny
'But I have seen Gary who does have a vanny.'
'But Gary does not have a pink vanny.'
And so that was the end of Aunt Fanny's vanny.

Madeline Fisher (9)
Whittle-Le-Woods CE Primary School

Horses

Horses are daft but gentle,
Run around like something mental,
Jump aboard, gallop around,
Maybe you will fall on the ground.

Groom them nice,
Check for lice,
Give them hay,
Suppertime put them in the nice warm bay
Maybe they will have a play,
Careful now, they don't want to fight,
Soon they will snuggle up for the night.

Now you're done
Go off and have some fun.

Georgina Russell (11)
Whittle-Le-Woods CE Primary School

My Friend

M y friend is Holly
Y ou make me happy

F riends make you have fun
R ich and dumb
I 'm happy and I'm having fun
E njoy it when we play
N ever have a bad day
D ays fly past.

Hannah Smith-Haughton (9)
Whittle-Le-Woods CE Primary School

Clayton Cup

Tracksuit on, all geared up
The night is here, it's Clayton Cup.

Into the room with our school name on the wall
The whistle was blown to start with netball.

Cricket up next, standing in a row,
We win with 20 hits, go Whittle go.

We pick up the rope and the man said go
We pull and we tug, but we lose *oh no.*

The team are happy and what a good pick
For those that are good with a hockey stick.

We dribble around the cones and there's cheers around the hall
Another five points, we win the football.

During the break the crowd let out a cheer
While my dad's in the bar having a pint of beer.

Into the sack, it's a relay race
At the finish they are all red in the face.

Over our heads went the big blue mat,
We're first past the cone and then we sat.

The last race of the night, our hearts are beating fast
The crowds are shouting, we need Manor Road to come last.

It's been such fun and we're dying with thirst
But a fabulous night, we came joint first!

April Bateman (11)
Whittle-Le-Woods CE Primary School

Ten Silly Children

(Based on 'Ten Little Schoolboys' by A A Milne)

Ten silly children
Drinking wine
One drank too much
Then there were nine.

Nine silly children
Playing with a mate
One ran away
And then there were eight.

Eight silly children
Playing up in Heaven
One fell down
And then there were seven.

Seven silly children
Mixing pips
One ate a rotten one
And then there were six.

Six silly children
Standing alive
Along came an alien
And then there were five.

Five silly children
Playing on the floor
The door began to shake
And then there were four.

Four silly children,
Saw a bee
The bee stung one
And then there were three.

Three silly children
Playing in the blue
The sky fell in
And then there were two.

Two silly children
Eating a scone
One was poisoned
And then there was one.

One silly child
Finished his scone
Along came a crocodile
And then there were none.

Alice Gregory (8)
Whittle-Le-Woods CE Primary School

Match Girls Strike

Match girls strike is important,
So important to us girls.

We are women,
We will fight.

We want hygiene and things like light
We want dental health and having fun with someone else.

We are women,
We will fight.

We want a raise a very big raise,
Seventeen shillings at least.

We are women,
We will fight.

We want to talk, let us
And we won't sue.

We are women,
We will fight.

Ben Lancaster (9)
Withnell Fold Primary School

Working In The Mill

Don't go down with your hair dangling out
Or you will get the whip.
Crawl under the machines and sweep up neat and tidy,
Be careful, don't catch your legs or your hair
Or you will get paid less.
You can't have a horse or carriage to take you home from work,
Get your money and pay the bills,
For the food you buy tonight.
Your family hopes
You'll get them full up.
For the morning they have less food.
Go to bed
And fall asleep
For a hard day tomorrow.

The morning has come
And they have had their share
Of the bread loaf that they had left,
From the big dinner last night.
Off to the factory
Where they are all working hard
To get money for the family
Someone with *phossyjaw*
Shouting for *help!*
End of the day
The day is gone
Go home for tea
And wait for the hard day tomorrow.

Natalie Toth (10)
Withnell Fold Primary School

The Smuggler

The ship's as black as midnight
As cold as a block of ice
They float in shallow waters
On the drifts of cold, rough seas

The boat's heavily loaded
The silence of the oars
The men are ever so cold
But they get over the waves

The sea was crashing onto the rocks
Lashing to the shore, lashing, lashing
Slapping against the boat
But they make it to the cave

The cave's well hidden entrance
Dark, damp and very, very old
Covered with green mould
They leave, but they'll return.

Elizabeth Jones (11)
Withnell Fold Primary School

A Hot Summer's Night

The sun sets overlooking the sand,
Beaming its rays upon the land
Like bolts of fire in angry pursuit
They stream straight out
Like music from a flute
The warmth of the light
In that cold summer's night
Makes me shiver, as the brightness grows
And my heart starts to quiver
As I bask in the hotness of that beaming sun
I reflect on the day and what is to come.

Shona Jackson (10)
Withnell Fold Primary School

The Night For The Smugglers

Smugglers are sailing in their ship
Going left and right
Going to a boat to collect beer
The ship's sails swishing
Forwards and backwards.

Small boats cutting through the water
To collect beer and coming back
To their ship with lots of goods.

The sea crashing against the smuggler's ship
Waves lashing between rocks
Waves lapping over each other
The large waves knocking the ship
From side to side.

The men sailing their boats towards a cave
As they come up very quietly
King George's men don't hear.

Natasha McMahon (10)
Withnell Fold Primary School

The Smugglers

The crashing of the waves
Sounded like thunder
The waves were lapping, like leaping horses
While the men were rowing up to the old, stony cave.

The ghostly ship was drifting
Waves were slapping against the ship
But the heavy loads inside
Were bobbing up and down.

As the smugglers' boat was being rowed
The old oars were pulling the hidden treasures
But if the moon lights their way
It won't stop the smugglers from still coming.

The old, damp, stony cave
Was full with barrels so high
But be careful where you go tonight
You might meet smugglers!

Bethany Wood (10)
Withnell Fold Primary School

Smugglers Poem

The crashing waves in a storm,
Slapping against each other, then going down again.
As dark as the midnight sky
The rough sea hitting the rocks.
Smash! And then smacking something hard.

Dark brown wood, covered with sea
White sails flapping in the wind.
Floating in deep seas
The ghostly sighs of someone on it
Watch out, there are the smugglers.

Silently from behind the ship
You can hear someone whispering, *'Pull, pull!'*
Hiding among the waves
Heavily loaded, full of goods
Then slowly floating up to the shore.

A cave so dark, you can't see
Taking the goods in
This dark and damp place
Full of valuable goods
The smugglers will wait and come again.

Ali Wrigley (10)
Withnell Fold Primary School

The Smugglers Song

The grand, gloomy ship floating in the moonlight,
Fighting through the low mist,
Stormy winds blowing against the larger sails,
Crashing upon the harbour walls
The little boats bobbing up and down.

As dark and gloomy as night
Ghostly galleons passing by,
Sails flapping in the cold winds
Floating in the deep, rough waters
Waves slapping against the sides.

As heavily loaded as an elephant
Hidden in the large waves
Laying low against the waves
Rocking on the waves
The smugglers row back to the shore.

Pitch-black caves
Old, jagged edges in the stone
Barrels behind the old, damp wood
Up against the wall
The smugglers' hoard is stored.

Carla Davy (9)
Withnell Fold Primary School

The Ghost Traveller

The wind was a roaring monster among the rustling grass,
Moon was a beam of light over the wavy mass,
The road was a river of shadows on the old, grassy moor
And ghost traveller came galloping, galloping
The ghost traveller came galloping up to the old castle door.

He had a battered, woollen hat on his head
And a white collar at his chin,
He had a dark jacket of leather, his pants were old bearskin,
They had not a crease in sight, his boots up to the knee,
His gold jewels shining,
His silver buckle shining,
The castle lights all that he could see.

Over the stones he clattered to the castle barn,
He hit his sword on the gates and looked over to the nearby farm
He shouted up to the window, and shouted her name
And the king's fair-haired daughter Jane,
The king's pretty daughter Jane,
The king's lovely daughter heard and she came.

Connor White (11)
Withnell Fold Primary School

The Smugglers' Adventure

The sea waves lapping over each other,
The strong wind blowing the sea one way,
Waves getting faster and faster
And the mist closing in on the salt water.

The ship crashing amongst the sea waves,
The wood gathering more water,
The sails flapping in the gusts of wind
And the boat with a ghost-like face.

The little boat heavily loaded,
Lying quietly on the violent waves,
The men whispering, keep rowing
As they go through the misty night sky.

The cave hidden in the moonlit sky,
Mist entering into the cave.
Pitch-black, nothing to be seen
Scary and horrifying.

Alex Snape (10)
Withnell Fold Primary School

Working At The Mill

I wake up every morning,
To hear the morning bell,
I look around the room,
So similar to a cell.

The mistress knocks on our door
And comes into the room,
She stubbornly awakens us,
By hitting us with a broom.

We all get up and dressed,
Ready for the mill,
With all the dust and cobwebs,
We could get very ill.

We all walk down the street,
Arriving for work today,
If we do our duty well,
We'll get our full pay.

Miss Shaw told us off,
For being late for work,
Beth's hair was out of her bonnet,
Miss Shaw, she went berserk.

Annie Miller (11)
Withnell Fold Primary School

The Smuggler Song

The waves crash against the shore,
The swirling waves lapping over an old broken door.
The waves are like horses galloping in the sea
And the rocks so spiky on the ground.

The giant ship sets off to sea,
On our way back from a foreign country.
We are halfway there to the secret beach,
Our ship is big and strong.

Our boat is small and weak,
I bet the brown paint will leak.
We sailed on and on and then we arrived,
We were all happy to have survived.

The cave is dark and gloomy,
It's damp and cold and scary
This is where we hide our gold
And the king's men are waiting.

Elisabeth Peck (9)
Withnell Fold Primary School

A Smuggler's Song

The wavy sea was crashing upon the dripping rocks,
The deep blue sea was lapping on the golden sand,
The rough sea lashing against the pebbles near the cave,
In the harbour the boats were bobbing up and down.

The ship was floating in shallow waters,
The smugglers came out,
As the sails were flapping in the rapid wind
You never hear anyone shout.

The rowing boat was heavily loaded,
With barrels and very heavy chests,
Then you hear a smuggler whisper,
'Pull, pull, pull, pull.'

Into the damp cave the smugglers went,
They went in the bat-infested cave,
But the king's men don't know
Where the treasure's stored.

Lauren Jaynes (9)
Withnell Fold Primary School

Smugglers Poem

The sea lapping on the seashore,
Crashing upon the rocks,
Splashing in the air,
The sea is as deep and dark as you could imagine,
Scary and frightening too.

The ship floating in the dark sea, blurred in the low mist,
The sails flapping to and fro,
The smuggler gang crowd the ship,
As thunder and lightning crack through the sky,
Slowly drifting towards our land.

The thin rowing boat glides through the jumpy waves,
Silently and softly the rowing boat heads towards the deep, dark cave,
Smugglers unload the goods and take them to the cave.

The mysterious cave is full of valuable goods,
The smugglers have found the perfect place to hide their treasures,
They all sit down and tell each other what a good job they have done.

Fionach Miller (9)
Withnell Fold Primary School

Smugglers

The rough sea is crashing against the shore
Lapping and slapping over the jagged rocks
The waves are like galloping horses leaping on top of each other
The sea is rough, the sea is very misty.

The ghostly ship floating over the low, cloudy sea
It bobs up an down, the sails flapping wildly
The smugglers silently rowing over the crashing sea
A smuggler silently whispers, 'Pull, pull and pull.'

The overloaded boat, lying in the waves,
The boat drifting through the mist, the moon shining brightly,
In the boat hundreds of noisy bottles, they try to make silent,
The boat is pulling quickly through the stormy sea.

The smugglers creep silently out of the boat
Carrying the bottles, they go towards the damp cave,
They had piles of bottles everywhere in the cold and damp cave
The cave was very cold, there were drops of water on the damp floor.

Kate Widdowson (10)
Withnell Fold Primary School

The Smugglers' Journey

Violent wind lashing through the waves,
Crashing fiercely against the rocky shore,
The smell of the salty sea air,
Waves lapping viciously over each other.

A misty silhouette moving slowly against the moonlight,
A rusty, creaking ship cutting through the waves,
Sails flapping wildly from side to side,
Swiftly travelling through the sea.

Battling against the rough sea,
Hidden beneath the waves,
Loaded with expensive goods,
Silently drifting into the mist.

Secretive and hidden amongst the shore,
Dark, gloomy and hollow, the cave where the smugglers hide,
Filled with the goods for the boat,
Footsteps echoing slightly as they carry in heavy barrels.

Danielle Jackson (11)
Withnell Fold Primary School

The Night Of The Smugglers

The sea crashing like a boulder in the wind,
The waves lapping on top of each other,
The boats by the harbour wall bobbing up and down,
Be careful where you go or you might meet the smugglers.

The ship floating in shallow waters,
Drifting along by night,
The white sails flapping
During the dark, stormy night.

The little, tiny rowing boat by the harbour,
With eight men whispering quietly.
'Row, row, row,' a man with a beard calls
Whilst the boat bobs among the waves.

People tiptoeing to the dark cave during the night,
Small, dark and gloomy, it's so scary.
Stacked high with goods to the roof,
People cackling quietly in the night sky.

Deborah Norris (10)
Withnell Fold Primary School

The Smugglers' Cave

Huge waves crashing into the shore lashing against the rocks,
Overlapping each other, jumping and diving,
Slipping down into the dark blue sea,
Up and down like giant leaping horses.

The ship floating in the dark sea, blurred in the low mist,
Waves throwing themselves at the rotted wood,
Wind blowing around at the huge sails,
The ghostly ship, black in the night sky.

The little rowing boat, heavily loaded with goods,
Waves rising so high the boat is hidden,
Silently drifting through the mist,
The boat nearly tipping over in the rough sea.

The cave, damp from when the sea was last at high tide,
Ancient rocks forming a huge cave,
Crumbling rocks falling away from the cave,
The cave is hidden in the black night sky.

James Hopkin (11)
Withnell Fold Primary School